Good Earth Almanac

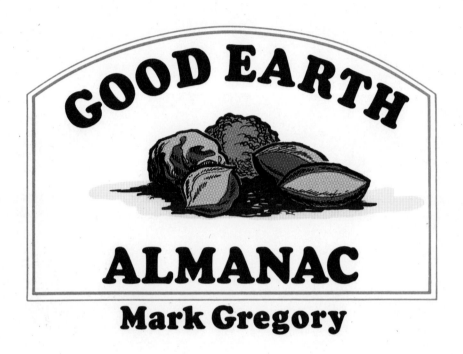

GOOD EARTH

ALMANAC

Mark Gregory

GROSSET & DUNLAP
A National General Company

Publishers   **New York**

Copyright © 1971, 1972, 1973 by Universal Press Syndicate
All rights reserved
Published simultaneously in Canada

Library of Congress Catalog Card Number: 72-90840
ISBN: 0-448-02038-6–paperback edition
ISBN: 0-448-01979-5–trade edition
ISBN: 0-448-03796-3—library edition

First printing

Printed in the United States of America

CONTENTS

INTRODUCTION

Today's plastic world is manufactured, packaged and handed to us; then we are taught or conditioned to believe that all of this artificiality is actually the best for us, regardless of the cost to body or spirit. But there are still a few people, most of them holdouts in the country, who believe in shaping their own destiny by living a more natural life. These people are fast being joined by others who, even though they are urban dwellers or are bound to the suburban treadmill, are gaining some feeling of independence through awareness of the natural world and of their own selves. That is what *Good Earth Almanac* is all about: a rediscovery of the natural world, with all its creatures and plants that surround us; and with awareness of the physical world, a reawakening of our own inner strengths.

My grandfather once told me that someday there would be children who would never see a cow, know where milk came from, taste a juicy ripe tomato pulled fresh from the vine and eaten on the spot or search the ripe spring woods for elusive mushrooms. As a child I thought this funny and impossible, but years later I found out how truly he spoke. Many people have lost contact with the real world. Living in a simulated world, they have lost the natural world of the good earth.

Everyone and everything has suffered from this loss, and today our rivers run red, blue, yellow and frothy with the results of our misunderstanding and misuse of our planet earth. But we are beginning to realize that we don't get something for nothing, and we are on our first giant step to restoring some of the damage. But the damage would never have been done if we hadn't been so alienated from the natural world in the first place. We have become so interested in acquiring more radios, television sets, automobiles, household appliances, any article at all just as long as it entertains us, that we have forgotten the real joys of life. We have forgotten what it feels like to lie on the fresh green grass of spring and watch the blue and white sky roll by us, a big red-tailed marsh hawk dipping and soaring with the air currents high above.

Man, the ultimate predator, does have a place in the natural world, and it is up to him to use his gift of intelligence to see that he plays his true role in the order of natural living.

I was one of the lucky ones, growing up with people around me who understood and loved the natural world and who knew the importance of passing valuable knowledge and crafts from generation to generation. I was taught how to identify trees and what wood makes the best fires, how to milk a cow and how to produce hay to feed her, how to use and enjoy and respect the good earth.

I owe a debt to all the people who have had the patience and taken the time to teach me the wonders of forest and field and some of the old almost forgotten but very important life-supporting crafts of our ancestors. I hope to repay this debt by passing along this valuable and hard-won knowledge to those who most appreciate it, and will use it to make their world a better and more natural place to live.

Mark Gregory

1
GATHERING

FOOD
IN THE WILD

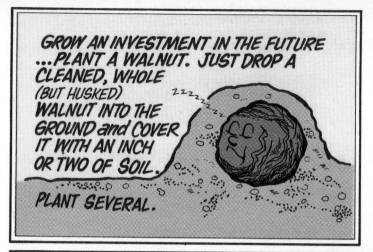

GROW AN INVESTMENT IN THE FUTURE ...PLANT A WALNUT. JUST DROP A CLEANED, WHOLE (BUT HUSKED) WALNUT INTO THE GROUND and COVER IT WITH AN INCH OR TWO OF SOIL.

PLANT SEVERAL.

NATURAL FOODS

NUTS WERE ONE OF THE FIRST FOODS FOR MAN. HICKORY NUTS AND PECANS ARE DELIGHTFUL IN CANDIES, PIES and COOKIES. NUTS ARE ALSO HEALTHFUL SNACKS.

NOTE: NOT ALL HICKORY NUTS ARE FLAVORFUL; SOME ARE VERY BITTER.

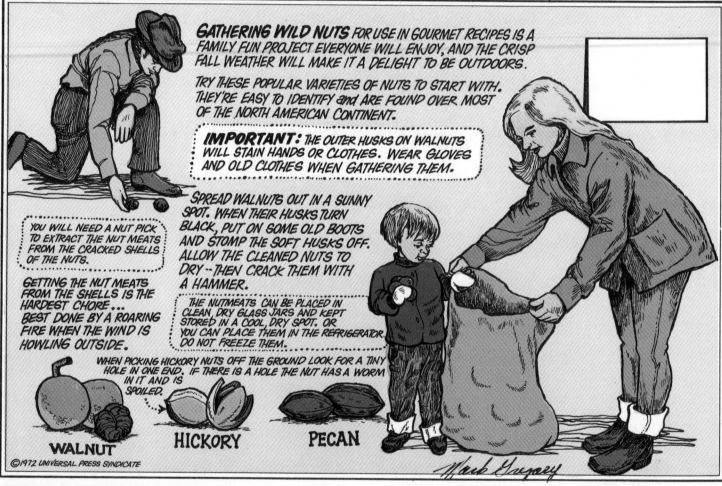

GATHERING WILD NUTS FOR USE IN GOURMET RECIPES IS A FAMILY FUN PROJECT EVERYONE WILL ENJOY, AND THE CRISP FALL WEATHER WILL MAKE IT A DELIGHT TO BE OUTDOORS.

TRY THESE POPULAR VARIETIES OF NUTS TO START WITH. THEY'RE EASY TO IDENTIFY and ARE FOUND OVER MOST OF THE NORTH AMERICAN CONTINENT.

IMPORTANT: THE OUTER HUSKS ON WALNUTS WILL STAIN HANDS OR CLOTHES. WEAR GLOVES AND OLD CLOTHES WHEN GATHERING THEM.

YOU WILL NEED A NUT PICK TO EXTRACT THE NUT MEATS FROM THE CRACKED SHELLS OF THE NUTS.

GETTING THE NUT MEATS FROM THE SHELLS IS THE HARDEST CHORE... BEST DONE BY A ROARING FIRE WHEN THE WIND IS HOWLING OUTSIDE.

SPREAD WALNUTS OUT IN A SUNNY SPOT. WHEN THEIR HUSKS TURN BLACK, PUT ON SOME OLD BOOTS AND STOMP THE SOFT HUSKS OFF. ALLOW THE CLEANED NUTS TO DRY -- THEN CRACK THEM WITH A HAMMER.

THE NUTMEATS CAN BE PLACED IN CLEAN, DRY GLASS JARS AND KEPT STORED IN A COOL, DRY SPOT. OR YOU CAN PLACE THEM IN THE REFRIGERATOR. DO NOT FREEZE THEM.

WHEN PICKING HICKORY NUTS OFF THE GROUND LOOK FOR A TINY HOLE IN ONE END. IF THERE IS A HOLE THE NUT HAS A WORM IN IT AND IS SPOILED.

WALNUT   HICKORY   PECAN

©1972 UNIVERSAL PRESS SYNDICATE

Mack Gregory

Natural Crafts

FOR TRULY UNUSUAL JEWELRY...

1. SLICE WALNUT SHELLS INTO THIN DISCS...

2. SHELLS MUST BE CLAMPED IN VISE OR PLIERS. CUT WITH JEWELERS SAW.

3. POLISH WITH SANDPAPER, THEN BRUSH ON SHELLAC.

4. GLUE TO EARRING MOUNT, TIE TACK, ETC. (AVAILABLE AT HOBBY SHOPS.)

JOIN WITH COPPER WIRE FOR BELTS, BRACELETS, ETC.

TANGLED PATCHES OF BLACKBERRY VINES ARE HOME TO ALL KINDS OF WILDLIFE.

AN EXCELLENT OLD-TIME PIE IS FRESH BLACKBERRY PIE. STIR 5 or 6 CUPS OF WASHED and DRAINED FRESHLY PICKED BLACKBERRIES IN WITH ¼ CUP OF HONEY. CHILL. TO SERVE; POUR INTO A PIE SHELL, WHIP 1 CUP OF HEAVY CREAM AND SPREAD OVER THE PIE.

Wild Blackberries

GROW IN ALMOST ALL PARTS OF THE U.S. and CANADA AND ARE ONE OF NATURE'S MOST DELICIOUS SWEET FRUITS. THEY ARE ENJOYED BY ALL KINDS OF WILDLIFE AS WELL AS MAN. HIGH IN VITAMIN C, THESE BERRIES ARE EASILY RECOGNIZED AND CAN NOT ONLY PROVIDE A DELICIOUS SNACK WHILE HIKING IN THE WOODS, BUT CAN SERVE AS A WINTER'S SUPPLY OF FRUIT FOR USE IN ALL SORTS OF WAYS.

DEPENDING ON THE LOCALITY AND WEATHER CONDITIONS, BLACKBERRIES START TO RIPEN IN LATE SPRING AND ARE USUALLY READY TO PICK BY EARLY SUMMER. ONCE YOU LOCATE A PATCH, WATCH IT CLOSELY BECAUSE THE MAJORITY OF BERRIES CAN RIPEN ALMOST OVERNIGHT AND QUICKLY BECOME SO RIPE AND JUICY, THEY START TO FALL OFF THE VINES.

GOOD BLACKBERRY PATCHES ARE FOUND IN SANDY, WELL-DRAINED AREAS. A GOOD SPOT TO LOOK FOR THEM IS AT THE EDGES OF WOODED CLEARINGS OR IN OVERGROWN FIELDS OF SANDY SOIL. ANOTHER GOOD SPOT IS AROUND OLD, FALLEN-DOWN HOMESTEADS.

BLACKBERRIES CAN BE PREPARED IN ANY NUMBER OF WAYS:

1. FOR FRESH BERRIES -- MERELY PICK, WASH AND EAT WITH LOTS OF COLD MILK or CREAM.

2. FROZEN BLACKBERRIES ARE GREAT TO EAT ALL WINTER. TO PREPARE FOR FREEZING; WASH, DRAIN, AND ADD A CUP OF SUGAR TO EACH QUART OF BERRIES. PLACE IN FREEZER CONTAINERS.

3. BLACKBERRIES CAN BE COOKED INTO A CUSTARD TYPE DESSERT THAT WILL SATISFY EVEN THE MOST DISCRIMINATING GOURMET. JUST MIX A QUART OF BERRIES WITH ABOUT A CUP OF WATER AND A CUP OF HONEY. BRING TO A BOIL AND SIMMER UNTIL BERRIES ARE SOFT. MIX 2 TABLESPOONS OF CORN STARCH WITH A LITTLE WATER AND ADD TO THICKEN THE JUICE. POUR INTO DESSERT CUPS AND CHILL.

4. AND, OF COURSE, BLACKBERRIES CAN BE USED IN PIES and COBBLERS, JELLIES, JAMS, WINES and CORDIALS.

Herb Gregory

Natural Crafts

IF YOU PLAN TO PICK MORE THAN A HANDFUL OF BLACKBERRIES YOU SHOULD DRESS PROPERLY.

WEAR OLD CLOTHES (LONG SLEEVES and PANTS) AND A GOOD HAT. A PAIL, ITS BAIL LOOPED THROUGH AN OLD BELT AROUND YOUR WAIST, WILL LEAVE BOTH HANDS FREE FOR FASTER PICKING.

WEARING OLD COTTON GLOVES WITH THE FINGERS CUT OUT WILL PROTECT YOUR HANDS FROM THE PRICKLY VINES, YET ENABLE YOU TO EASILY PICK THE BERRIES.

RIPE PERSIMMONS ARE A "GOURMET TREAT" FOR WILDLIFE AND ARE ENJOYED BY ALMOST EVERYTHING THAT WALKS, CRAWLS OR FLIES.

NATURAL FOODS

THE DRIED PERSIMMON LEAVES MAKE AN EXCELLENT TEA. THE LEAVES ARE SAID TO BE HIGH IN VITAMIN C AND THE TEA WAS USED IN OLDEN TIMES TO HELP PREVENT SCURVY.

THE PERSIMMON, ONE OF THE MOST DELICIOUS FRUITS IN NORTH AMERICA, GROWS WILD AND IS FREE FOR THE GATHERING. IGNORED BY MANY PEOPLE, THIS SUCCULENT FRUIT IS CALLED "SUGAR PLUM" BY THOSE WHO HAVE TASTED ITS FULL SWEET FLAVOR.

PERSIMMONS ARE FOUND AT THE EDGES OF WOODS, ROADSIDES, ALONG CREEK BANKS AND IN ABANDONED FIELDS AND ABANDONED HOMESTEADS. A GREAT PERSIMMON HUNTING AREA IS AN ABANDONED WASTELAND THAT HAS GROWN OVER IN BRUSH AND SHRUBS.

TO BE EDIBLE, A PERSIMMON MUST BE "MUSHY" RIPE; A PERSIMMON THAT IS NOT QUITE RIPE IS SO BITTER IT WILL LEAVE YOU PUCKERED UP FOR A WEEK. DEAD RIPE PERSIMMONS ARE SO SOFT AND FRAGILE THEY WILL ALMOST MELT IN YOUR MOUTH, AND WILL FALL FROM THE TREE AT THE SLIGHTEST TOUCH.

RIPE PERSIMMONS ARE A PINKISH ORANGE, THE FRUIT BEING ABOUT AN INCH TO INCH AND A HALF IN DIAMETER AND FILLED WITH A JUICY ORANGE PULP AND FROM 2 TO 6 LARGE SEEDS.

PERSIMMONS START TO RIPEN ABOUT THE LAST OF SEPTEMBER AND MANY WILL STAY ON THE TREE UNTIL THE MIDDLE OF WINTER.

PERSIMMONS CAN MERELY BE PICKED OFF THE TREE, BUT A GREAT WAY OF HARVESTING A LARGE AMOUNT IS TO PLACE A SHEET ON THE GROUND UNDER THE TREE, AND SHAKE THE TREE. BUT MAKE SURE YOU CHECK EACH INDIVIDUAL FRUIT TO INSURE THAT IT IS RIPE.

THE EASIEST WAY TO ENJOY A PERSIMMON IS TO MERELY PICK AND EAT AS YOU WALK THROUGH THE WOODS, BUT IF YOU WANT TO KEEP SOME FOR LATER USE, YOU'LL HAVE TO MASH THE FRUIT AND EXTRACT THE PULP FROM THE SEEDS AND SKINS. THIS PULP MAY THEN BE FROZEN AND KEPT IN A FREEZER, OR DRIED FOR LATER USE. PIECES BROKEN OFF TASTE LIKE CANDY, AND MAY BE ADDED TO BREADS OR CEREAL.

Natural Crafts

ONE OF THE EASIEST WAYS OF PRESERVING PERSIMMONS WAS USED BY THE INDIANS. THEY DRIED PERSIMMONS IN THE SUN ON A FLAT ROCK OR CLEAN LOG. YOU CAN DO THE SAME, ONLY USING AN OVEN FOR DRYING.

1. SPREAD THE PULP OUT ON A COOKIE SHEET.

2. DRY IN OVEN SET AT LOW HEAT UNTIL PULP IS LEATHER-HARD.

3. REMOVE FROM OVEN AND STORE IN CLEAN, DRY, GLASS JARS.

MANY PEOPLE HAVE GONE HUNGRY WITH MILLIONS OF WILD GREENS GROWING ALL AROUND THEM "FREE FOR THE PICKING."

WILD GREENS PROVIDE AS MUCH OR MORE FLAVOR and NUTRITION AS THEIR COUSIN, THE WELL KNOWN SPINACH, AND USUALLY WITHOUT QUITE SO MUCH ARGUMENT FROM THE FAMILY.

TO MANY PEOPLE "PICKIN' GREENS" IS A SPRING RITUAL THAT PROVIDES NOT ONLY DELICIOUS EATING, BUT A CHANCE TO ENJOY THE OUTDOORS AT ITS BEST. THERE ARE HUNDREDS OF VARIETIES OF WILD GREENS GROWING ALL OVER THE WORLD, AND SOME OF THEM GROW ALL YEAR ROUND. THE FOUR GREENS SHOWN HERE ARE SOME OF THE MOST COMMON AND EASILY RECOGNIZED. IN FACT, MOST WILD GREENS YOU WILL RECOGNIZE AS PESKY WEEDS THAT PERSIST IN GROWING IN YOUR LAWN OR GARDEN. OTHER GOOD SPOTS FOR "GREENS" ARE VACANT LOTS AND RURAL ROADSIDES.

MUSTARD (BRASSICA)

THIS WELL KNOWN PLANT GROWS THE WORLD OVER AND NOT ONLY CAN PROVIDE LOTS OF DELICIOUS GREENS, BUT PRE-PARED MUSTARD AS WELL. IT BELONGS TO THE RADISH, CABBAGE, and TURNIP FAMILY. THE YOUNG LEAVES OF THE MUSTARD FAMILY ARE DELICIOUS ADDED TO A SALAD. THEY ADD A SLIGHTLY "MUSTARDY" FLAVOR. MUSTARD GREENS PREPARED BY COOKING REQUIRE A BIT MORE COOKING THAN MOST OTHER GREENS.

LAMBS QUARTERS (CHENOPODIUM)

CALLED WILD SPINACH BY MANY PEOPLE, THIS IS THE MILDEST TASTING OF WILD GREENS. THE TEN-DER TOP LEAVES OF THE PLANT CAN BE EATEN FROM EARLY SPRING THROUGHOUT THE SUMMER. GROWING ALL OVER THE UNITED STATES AND CANADA, THIS GREEN BELONGS TO THE SPINACH AND BEET FAMILY. IT IS DELICIOUS EITHER RAW OR COOKED. FOR RAW SALAD, SERVE WITH VINEGAR AND OIL DRESSING. WHEN COOKING, COOK OVER A LOW HEAT JUST UNTIL GREENS BECOME "LIMP", THEN SERVE WITH A BIG PATTY OF BUTTER.

SHEPHERD'S PURSE (CAPSELLA)

GROWING IN A LOOSE ROSETTE CLOSE TO THE GROUND AND MUCH LIKE A DANDELION, THIS GREEN SHOOTS FORTH LONG SPINDLY STEMS WITH TINY HEART-SHAPED SEED PODS, POINTS DOWN. IS FOUND MOST EVERYWHERE AND IS GENERALLY AVAILABLE FOR MOST OF THE YEAR. TENDER YOUNG LEAVES ARE DELI-CIOUS PREPARED AS A SALAD WITH TOMATO WEDGES AND YOUR FAVORITE DRESSING. OLDER LEAVES CAN BE COOKED IN SALTED WATER UNTIL LIMP, THEN SERVED WITH VINEGAR AND A HARD-BOILED EGG.

DOCK (RUMEX)

THIS IS ONE OF THE MOST COMMON AND HEARTY OF GREENS. IT GROWS ALL OVER THE U.S. AND CANADA AND HAS A DOZEN DIFFERENT VARIETIES. THIS PLANT IS A BIT TOUGHER, REQUIRING MORE COOKING, AND IS MORE BITTER THAN OTHER GREENS. DOES NOT MAKE A VERY GOOD SALAD. SHOULD BE BOILED IN SALTED WATER AND SERVED WITH A PATTY OF BUTTER.

Mark Gregory

Natural Crafts

WILD GREENS CAN EASILY BE FROZEN AND STORED FOR USE DURING THE OFF-SEASON MONTHS, PROVIDING A MUCH APPRECIATED VARIETY OF "VEGETABLE" DURING THE LONG WINTER MONTHS.

TO FREEZE GREENS, CLEAN AND PICK OVER YOUNG, TENDER LEAVES. BLANCH 2 MINUTES IN BOILING WATER, STIRRING TO KEEP LEAVES SEPARATED. COOL AND DRAIN THOROUGHLY AND PLACE IN FREEZER PACKAGES IMMEDIATELY.

THE INDIANS BOILED THE FLOWERS OF THE MILKWEED TO PRODUCE A SUGAR OR SYRUP.

NATURAL FOODS

MILKWEED PODS CAN BE EASILY FROZEN AND SAVED FOR OFF-SEASON USE. BOIL THEM IN THREE CHANGES OF WATER, THEN PACK IN FREEZER CONTAINERS. THEY SHOULD BE COOKED 15 TO 20 MINUTES BEFORE SERVING.

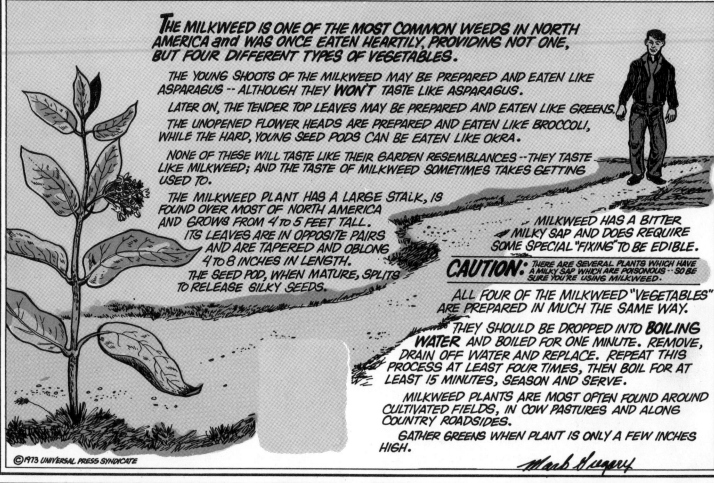

THE MILKWEED IS ONE OF THE MOST COMMON WEEDS IN NORTH AMERICA and WAS ONCE EATEN HEARTILY, PROVIDING NOT ONE, BUT FOUR DIFFERENT TYPES OF VEGETABLES.

THE YOUNG SHOOTS OF THE MILKWEED MAY BE PREPARED AND EATEN LIKE ASPARAGUS -- ALTHOUGH THEY WON'T TASTE LIKE ASPARAGUS.

LATER ON, THE TENDER TOP LEAVES MAY BE PREPARED AND EATEN LIKE GREENS.

THE UNOPENED FLOWER HEADS ARE PREPARED AND EATEN LIKE BROCCOLI, WHILE THE HARD, YOUNG SEED PODS CAN BE EATEN LIKE OKRA.

NONE OF THESE WILL TASTE LIKE THEIR GARDEN RESEMBLANCES -- THEY TASTE LIKE MILKWEED; AND THE TASTE OF MILKWEED SOMETIMES TAKES GETTING USED TO.

THE MILKWEED PLANT HAS A LARGE STALK, IS FOUND OVER MOST OF NORTH AMERICA AND GROWS FROM 4 TO 5 FEET TALL. ITS LEAVES ARE IN OPPOSITE PAIRS AND ARE TAPERED AND OBLONG 4 TO 8 INCHES IN LENGTH. THE SEED POD, WHEN MATURE, SPLITS TO RELEASE SILKY SEEDS.

MILKWEED HAS A BITTER MILKY SAP AND DOES REQUIRE SOME SPECIAL "FIXING" TO BE EDIBLE.

CAUTION: THERE ARE SEVERAL PLANTS WHICH HAVE A MILKY SAP WHICH ARE POISONOUS -- SO BE SURE YOU'RE USING MILKWEED.

ALL FOUR OF THE MILKWEED "VEGETABLES" ARE PREPARED IN MUCH THE SAME WAY.

THEY SHOULD BE DROPPED INTO BOILING WATER AND BOILED FOR ONE MINUTE. REMOVE, DRAIN OFF WATER AND REPLACE. REPEAT THIS PROCESS AT LEAST FOUR TIMES, THEN BOIL FOR AT LEAST 15 MINUTES, SEASON AND SERVE.

MILKWEED PLANTS ARE MOST OFTEN FOUND AROUND CULTIVATED FIELDS, IN COW PASTURES AND ALONG COUNTRY ROADSIDES.

GATHER GREENS WHEN PLANT IS ONLY A FEW INCHES HIGH.

Mark Gregory

© 1973 UNIVERSAL PRESS SYNDICATE

Natural Crafts

MILKWEED WAS CULTIVATED AND GROWN DURING WORLD WAR II. THE DOWN SEEDS WERE USED TO STUFF LIFE JACKETS.

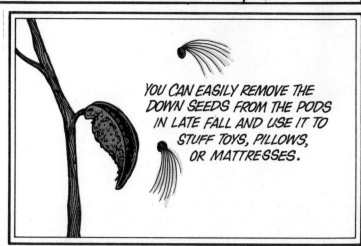

YOU CAN EASILY REMOVE THE DOWN SEEDS FROM THE PODS IN LATE FALL AND USE IT TO STUFF TOYS, PILLOWS, OR MATTRESSES.

POKEWEED IS OFTEN CALLED INKBERRY AND THE BRIGHT PURPLE JUICE OF THE BERRIES MAKES A VERY GOOD WRITING INK.

NATURAL FOODS

MANY PEOPLE LIKE POKE WITH OTHER GREENS SUCH AS "DOCK" OR "MUSTARD."

CURLEY DOCK

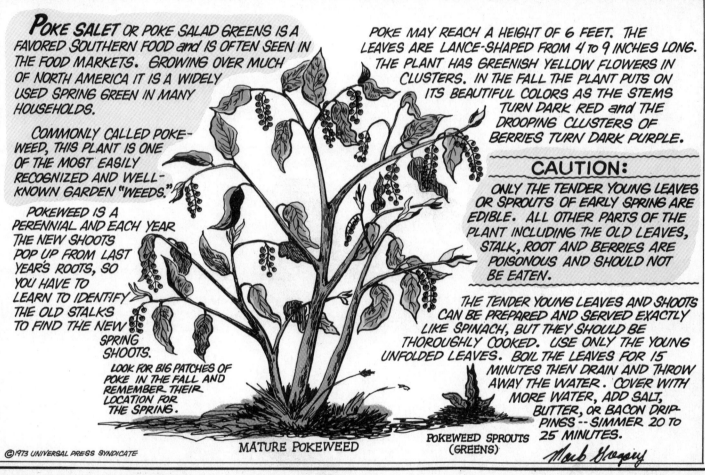

POKE SALET OR POKE SALAD GREENS IS A FAVORED SOUTHERN FOOD and IS OFTEN SEEN IN THE FOOD MARKETS. GROWING OVER MUCH OF NORTH AMERICA IT IS A WIDELY USED SPRING GREEN IN MANY HOUSEHOLDS.

COMMONLY CALLED POKEWEED, THIS PLANT IS ONE OF THE MOST EASILY RECOGNIZED AND WELL-KNOWN GARDEN "WEEDS."

POKEWEED IS A PERENNIAL AND EACH YEAR THE NEW SHOOTS POP UP FROM LAST YEAR'S ROOTS, SO YOU HAVE TO LEARN TO IDENTIFY THE OLD STALKS TO FIND THE NEW SPRING SHOOTS.

LOOK FOR BIG PATCHES OF POKE IN THE FALL AND REMEMBER THEIR LOCATION FOR THE SPRING.

© 1973 UNIVERSAL PRESS SYNDICATE

MATURE POKEWEED

POKE MAY REACH A HEIGHT OF 6 FEET. THE LEAVES ARE LANCE-SHAPED FROM 4 TO 9 INCHES LONG. THE PLANT HAS GREENISH YELLOW FLOWERS IN CLUSTERS. IN THE FALL THE PLANT PUTS ON ITS BEAUTIFUL COLORS AS THE STEMS TURN DARK RED and THE DROOPING CLUSTERS OF BERRIES TURN DARK PURPLE.

CAUTION:

ONLY THE TENDER YOUNG LEAVES OR SPROUTS OF EARLY SPRING ARE EDIBLE. ALL OTHER PARTS OF THE PLANT INCLUDING THE OLD LEAVES, STALK, ROOT AND BERRIES ARE POISONOUS AND SHOULD NOT BE EATEN.

THE TENDER YOUNG LEAVES AND SHOOTS CAN BE PREPARED AND SERVED EXACTLY LIKE SPINACH, BUT THEY SHOULD BE THOROUGHLY COOKED. USE ONLY THE YOUNG UNFOLDED LEAVES. BOIL THE LEAVES FOR 15 MINUTES THEN DRAIN AND THROW AWAY THE WATER. COVER WITH MORE WATER, ADD SALT, BUTTER, OR BACON DRIPPINGS -- SIMMER 20 TO 25 MINUTES.

POKEWEED SPROUTS (GREENS)

Marb Gregory

Natural Crafts

POKEWEED MAY EASILY BE PREPARED FOR WINTER USE BY BOILING FOR 10 MINUTES THEN PLACING IN FREEZER CONTAINERS AND FREEZING.

OR -- YOU CAN USE THE TENDER LEAVES JUST AS YOU WOULD SPINACH.

DON'T SPRAY GARDEN AND LAWN WEEDS. PULL THEM AND USE THEM IN YOUR COMPOST PILE.

The DANDELION WAS ONCE A HIGHLY TOUTED HEALTH HERB. THE VITAMIN-FILLED FRESH YOUNG LEAVES WERE EATEN RAW AS A POPULAR **SPRING TONIC**

GATHERING **WILD PLANTS** FOR FOOD IS FUN THAT CAN BE ENJOYED BY EVERYONE. ONE OF THE MOST POPULAR WILD PLANTS, AND THE FIRST TO ANNOUNCE SPRING TO THE FOOD FORAGER, IS THE LOWLY DANDELION. DANDELIONS ARE AN EXTREMELY DELICIOUS AND VERSATILE FOOD PLANT, BUT THEY MUST BE HARVESTED VERY EARLY IN THE SPRING.

JUST AS SOON AS THE FIRST WARM SPRING DAYS NUDGE THE YOUNG DANDELION LEAVES OUT OF THE GROUND, START PICKING THEM FOR GREENS. POP OFF THE LEAVES AT THEIR BASE AND SHAKE OUT ALL DIRT AND GRIT. RINSE OFF AND PLACE THE GREENS IN A PAN AND COVER WITH WATER. BOIL FOR ABOUT 7 MINUTES. PLACE A PATTY OF BUTTER ON EACH SERVING AND SALT AND PEPPER TO TASTE FOR A DELICIOUS MEAL OF DANDELION GREENS.

© 1972 Universal Press Syndicate

FOR A RATHER UNUSUAL VEGETABLE PULL THE ENTIRE PLANT. BETWEEN THE GREEN LEAVES AND THE ROOTS IS THE CROWN OF THE PLANT. CUT OFF THE LEAVES AND THE ROOT. WASH THE CROWN THOROUGHLY TO REMOVE ANY DIRT -- THEN BOIL IT FOR ABOUT 10 MINUTES. SERVE PIPING HOT WITH MELTED CHEESE AND SEASONED TO TASTE.

RAW DANDELION LEAVES CAN ALSO BE USED IN A GREEN SALAD --MIXED WITH LETTUCE. BUT USE THEM SPARINGLY, AS THE UNCOOKED LEAVES TEND TO BE BITTER.

DANDELION COFFEE. YOU CAN ALSO MAKE A SPECIAL "COFFEE" FROM THE LOWER DANDELION ROOTS. SCRUB THE ROOTS CLEAN, THEN CUT INTO TINY BITE-SIZED CHUNKS. PLACE THESE CHUNKS INTO A PAN AND ROAST IN A 300° OVEN FOR THREE OR FOUR HOURS (until they become crumbly). GRIND THESE ROOTS INTO A COARSE POWDER USING A BLENDER. OR YOU CAN BEAT THEM INTO CRUMBS WITH A ROLLING PIN OR POTATO MASHER. TO MAKE ONE SERVING OF COFFEE PLACE ONE TEASPOON OF THE POWDERED ROOTS INTO A CUP OF WATER AND BOIL FOR 5 MINUTES. POUR IN A TEASPOON OF COLD WATER TO SETTLE THE GROUNDS. --SWEETEN TO TASTE.

AFTER THE FLOWER BLOSSOMS, THE DANDELION PLANT BECOMES TOO BITTER TO BE EATEN. HOWEVER, THE FLOWER ITSELF IS USED BY MANY TO MAKE A LIGHT AND DELICIOUS "DANDELION WINE."

WARNING: USE **NO PLANTS** THAT HAVE BEEN SPRAYED WITH POISONS.

Natural Crafts

MAKING BARK **RUBBINGS** IS AN EASY WAY FOR YOUNGSTERS TO LEARN TO IDENTIFY TREES WITHOUT HAVING TO CUT OFF A SECTION FOR HOME STUDY.

WALNUT

BARK RUBBINGS ARE EASY TO MAKE. JUST PLACE A CLEAN PAPER OVER AN INTERESTING SECTION OF THE TREE BARK. HOLDING THE PAPER FIRMLY IN PLACE, RUB OVER ITS SURFACE WITH A WIDE PIECE OF COLORED CRAYON OR CHALK. THE PATTERN OF THE BARK WILL "PICK UP" THE COLORED CHALK ON THE PAPER.

THE ELDER PLANT WAS ONCE THOUGHT OF AS A CHARM IN SCANDINAVIAN COUNTRIES AND WAS PLACED OVER WINDOWS AND DOORS TO DRIVE AWAY EVIL SPIRITS AND WITCHES.

NATURAL FOODS

FOR A TRULY UNUSUAL NATURAL FOOD TRY BATTER-FRIED ELDERBERRY BLOSSOMS.

DIP THE WHOLE ELDERBERRY FLOWER IN YOUR FAVORITE LIGHT BATTER AND DROP IN HOT OIL.

WHEN CRISP AND BROWN, REMOVE AND DRIZZLE HONEY OVER THEM.

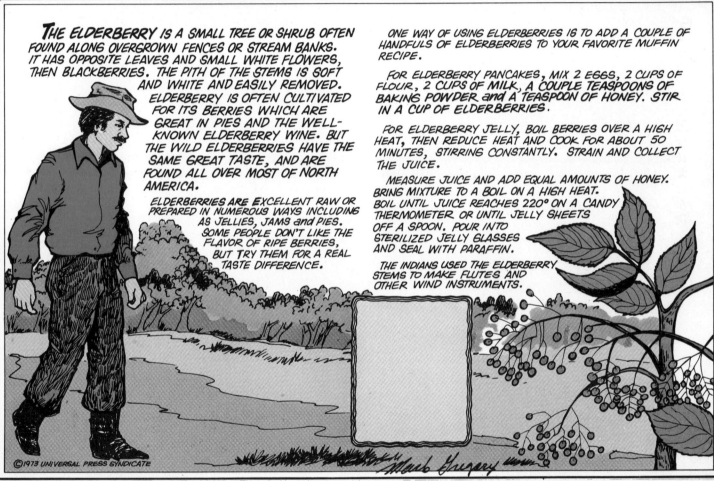

THE ELDERBERRY IS A SMALL TREE OR SHRUB OFTEN FOUND ALONG OVERGROWN FENCES OR STREAM BANKS. IT HAS OPPOSITE LEAVES AND SMALL WHITE FLOWERS, THEN BLACKBERRIES. THE PITH OF THE STEMS IS SOFT AND WHITE AND EASILY REMOVED. ELDERBERRY IS OFTEN CULTIVATED FOR ITS BERRIES WHICH ARE GREAT IN PIES AND THE WELL-KNOWN ELDERBERRY WINE. BUT THE WILD ELDERBERRIES HAVE THE SAME GREAT TASTE, AND ARE FOUND ALL OVER MOST OF NORTH AMERICA.

ELDERBERRIES ARE EXCELLENT RAW OR PREPARED IN NUMEROUS WAYS INCLUDING AS JELLIES, JAMS and PIES. SOME PEOPLE DON'T LIKE THE FLAVOR OF RIPE BERRIES, BUT TRY THEM FOR A REAL TASTE DIFFERENCE.

ONE WAY OF USING ELDERBERRIES IS TO ADD A COUPLE OF HANDFULS OF ELDERBERRIES TO YOUR FAVORITE MUFFIN RECIPE.

FOR ELDERBERRY PANCAKES, MIX 2 EGGS, 2 CUPS OF FLOUR, 2 CUPS OF MILK, A COUPLE TEASPOONS OF BAKING POWDER and A TEASPOON OF HONEY. STIR IN A CUP OF ELDERBERRIES.

FOR ELDERBERRY JELLY, BOIL BERRIES OVER A HIGH HEAT, THEN REDUCE HEAT AND COOK FOR ABOUT 50 MINUTES, STIRRING CONSTANTLY. STRAIN AND COLLECT THE JUICE.

MEASURE JUICE AND ADD EQUAL AMOUNTS OF HONEY. BRING MIXTURE TO A BOIL ON A HIGH HEAT. BOIL UNTIL JUICE REACHES 220° ON A CANDY THERMOMETER OR UNTIL JELLY SHEETS OFF A SPOON. POUR INTO STERILIZED JELLY GLASSES AND SEAL WITH PARAFFIN.

THE INDIANS USED THE ELDERBERRY STEMS TO MAKE FLUTES AND OTHER WIND INSTRUMENTS.

©1973 UNIVERSAL PRESS SYNDICATE

Natural Crafts

ELDERBERRIES ARE GREAT WHEN DRIED, TOO.

1. COLLECT FULLY RIPE BERRIES and STEM.

2. DRY ON FLAT SCREENS.

3. BOIL AND USE IN RECIPES CALLING FOR BLUEBERRIES.

MOREL MUSHROOMS GROW IN THE SAME AREA YEAR AFTER YEAR UNLESS THE SOIL IS DISTURBED. SO, IF YOU FIND A GOOD "MUSHROOM PATCH," IT WILL ANNUALLY PROVIDE A LOT OF DELICIOUS EATING.

MOREL MUSHROOMS CONTAIN NO CALORIES, AND AN EXCELLENT WAY TO PREPARE THEM IS TO DIP THE MUSHROOM PIECES IN BEATEN EGG YOLKS, THEN IN FLOUR AND DEEP FRY THEM IN HOT VEGETABLE OIL.

AN **OLD-TIME** SPRING TRADITION FOR MANY PEOPLE IS THE ANNUAL SEARCH FOR EDIBLE MUSHROOMS SUCH AS THE "MORELS," AND THIS IS ONE SPORT THAT DOESN'T REQUIRE A LICENSE, EXPENSIVE EQUIPMENT, NOR AN EXOTIC LOCALITY. IF THE HUNTER IS LUCKY HE'LL END UP WITH THE MAKINGS OF A GOURMET'S DELIGHT.

MORELS ARE AN EDIBLE MUSHROOM WHICH GROWS OVER MOST OF THE U.S. AND PARTS OF CANADA, AND ARE SOMETIMES CALLED "SPONGE" MUSHROOMS, BECAUSE THEY GREATLY RESEMBLE MINIATURE SPONGES. GROWING FROM 2 to 4 INCHES IN HEIGHT, THESE MUSHROOMS MAY BE PALE CREAM, BROWN or EVEN GRAY IN COLOR.

MORELS ARE THE AMATEUR MUSHROOM HUNTER'S DELIGHT, BECAUSE THEY ARE EASILY IDENTIFIED and DISTINGUISHED FROM POISONOUS MUSHROOMS, INCLUDING THE FALSE MOREL (helvella esculenta). TRUE MORELS HAVE A PITTED-POCKED SURFACE AS SHOWN. FALSE MORELS HAVE A CONVOLUTED SURFACE THAT RESEMBLES BRAIN TISSUE, AS ILLUSTRATED ABOVE.

CAUTION CARRY A GOOD MUSHROOM FIELD GUIDE BOOK (AVAILABLE AT ALL LEADING BOOK STORES) WITH YOU WHEN COLLECTING MUSHROOMS AND <u>MAKE SURE</u> YOU KNOW WHAT YOU'RE PICKING.

TRUE MOREL

FALSE MOREL

Mack Gregory

WHERE TO FIND MORELS: MORELS CAN BE FOUND IN THE DEEPEST WOODS - OR YOUR BACKYARD. THEY WILL BE LOCATED WHERE THERE IS A RICH, AERATED SOIL WITH A HIGH AMOUNT OF HUMUS. THEY REQUIRE DAMP CONDITIONS TO GROW and THRIVE. LOOK FOR THEM IN SPONGY SOIL NEAR CREEKS or IN OLD OVERGROWN APPLE OR PEACH ORCHARDS.

WHEN: MORELS START TO POP OUT ABOUT THE LAST OF APRIL and RUN THROUGH MOST OF MAY, DEPENDING ON WEATHER CONDITIONS. THE BEST TIME TO GO MOREL HUNTING IS ON A HOT, SUNNY AFTERNOON, FOLLOWING A MORNING RAIN SHOWER. MORELS SEEM TO POP UP ALL OVER THE WOODS ON SUCH A DAY.

MORELS MAY BE FRIED, ADDED TO SCRAMBLED EGGS OR USED IN SUCH GOURMET DELIGHTS AS "STUFFED MORELS" WITH HAMBURGER, AND WILL HAVE YOUR ENTIRE FAMILY ASKING FOR MORE.

It's Better to be Safe than Sorry.

TO KEEP MOREL MUSHROOMS, FOR EATING AFTER THEIR SHORT GROWING SEASON, YOU CAN DRY OR FREEZE THEM.

TO DRY, PLACE IN AN OVEN AT LOWEST TEMPERATURE, WITH DOOR OPEN, AND LEAVE UNTIL CRISP. PLACE IN A CLEAN, DRY JAR.

TO FREEZE, CUT IN HALF, WASH THOROUGHLY, BLOT OFF MOISTURE, PLACE IN FREEZER CONTAINERS.

PRODUCING **WASTE** IS MAN'S WAY... NOT NATURE'S.

MARSH MUFFINS

A GREAT TASTING RECIPE WITH CATTAIL POLLEN IS "MARSH MUFFINS." MERELY SUBSTITUTE HALF POLLEN FOR FLOUR IN YOUR FAVORITE MUFFIN RECIPE.

CATTAILS ARE EASILY ONE OF THE MOST VERSATILE **FOOD PLANTS.** THEY CAN PROVIDE VEGETABLE, SALAD AND EVEN "FLOUR". FOUND THROUGHOUT THE UNITED STATES, EXCEPT IN EXTREMELY DRY AREAS, THEY ARE A FORAGER'S DELIGHT, AND WILL PROVIDE FOOD FOR MOST OF THE YEAR.

VERY EARLY IN THE SPRING THE NEW LEAVES START TO SPROUT, AND THESE TINY STALKS AND LEAVES GREATLY RESEMBLE ASPARAGUS. IN FACT, THEY'RE CALLED *COSSACK ASPARAGUS* BY SOME, AND MAY BE PULLED AND EATEN FRESH *(IF THE WATER THEY'RE GROWING IN IS POLLUTION FREE).* JUST PULL OUT A STALK AND START EATING ON THE CRISPY WHITE STEM. THESE CAN ALSO BE GATHERED AND COOKED IN THE SAME MANNER YOU WOULD ASPARAGUS.

ANOTHER DELICIOUS PART OF THE CATTAIL PLANT IS A LUMP ABOUT THE SIZE OF A POTATO, AND LOCATED WHERE THE STEMS JOIN THE ROOTS. TO GET AT THIS TASTY VEGETABLE, RUN YOUR HAND DOWN INTO THE WATER UNTIL YOU FEEL THE ROOTS, THEN GIVE A MIGHTY HEAVE. PEEL AND BOIL THIS PART OF THE PLANT JUST LIKE POTATOES. TASTES SOMEWHAT LIKE A POTATO, BUT WITH ITS OWN "WILD" FLAVOR.

ABOUT THE LAST PART OF SPRING, IF YOU'RE WATCHING CLOSELY, YOU WILL SEE BLOOM SPIKES EMERGING ON THE STEMS. PICK THESE WHEN THEY REACH 4 OR 5 INCHES IN LENGTH. THESE TINY SPIKES ARE JUST LIKE EARS OF CORN, AND SHOULD BE PREPARED AND EATEN IN THAT MANNER. HUSK OFF THE OUTER LEAVES AND DROP THE SPIKES INTO BOILING WATER *(WELL SALTED).*

BOIL FOR ABOUT 10 MINUTES, THEN EAT LIKE CORN ON THE COB WITH PLENTY OF BUTTER AND SEASONING.

CATTAIL POLLEN IS ANOTHER EXCELLENT TASTING WILD FOOD. THIS GIVES EVERYTHING YOU ADD TO IT A BUTTER-LIKE COLOR AND A DELICIOUS CORN FLAVOR. CATTAIL POLLEN CAN BE SUBSTITUTED FOR FLOUR IN MANY RECIPES.

TO GATHER POLLEN, PLACE A PAPER OVER TOP A CLEAN BUCKET, CUT A SLOT IN THE PAPER, PUSH THE POLLEN LADEN SPIKES INTO THE BUCKET AND SHAKE.

Natural Crafts

LATER IN THE YEAR, THE COTTON OR DOWN FROM THE CATTAIL HEADS MAKES EXCELLENT FILLING FOR PILLOWS, FEATHERBEDS, ETC. WAS ONCE USED AS A LIFE-JACKET FILLING.

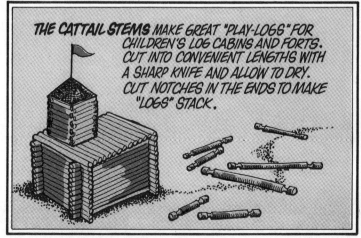

THE CATTAIL STEMS MAKE GREAT "PLAY-LOGS" FOR CHILDREN'S LOG CABINS AND FORTS. CUT INTO CONVENIENT LENGTHS WITH A SHARP KNIFE AND ALLOW TO DRY. CUT NOTCHES IN THE ENDS TO MAKE "LOGS" STACK.

IN ORDER TO MAKE A TABLESPOON OF HONEY, A BEE MUST VISIT ABOUT 2,000 FLOWERS.

NATURAL FOODS

HONEY IS A NATURAL NECTAR COLLECTED FROM FLOWERS. WHEN SUBSTITUTED FOR SUGAR IN RECIPES A CUP OF HONEY REPLACES A CUP OF SUGAR.

CLOVER HONEY

BEEKEEPING IS A HOBBY THAT CAN BE ENJOYED BY THE ENTIRE FAMILY. KEEPING BEES IS NOT ONLY INTERESTING AND EDUCATIONAL BUT THE BEES WILL PROVIDE YOUR FAMILY WITH THE MOST NATURAL SWEETENER -- LOTS OF GOLDEN, SWEET-SMELLING HONEY.

GETTING STARTED IN BEEKEEPING IS EASY AND NOT PARTICULARLY EXPENSIVE.

THE BEGINNING BEEKEEPER SHOULD NOT ATTEMPT TO START WITH MORE THAN ONE COLONY OF BEES.

THE MOST IMPORTANT PIECE OF EQUIPMENT IS THE BEEHIVE. THE BEST HIVE FOR THE BEGINNING "APIARIST" OR BEEKEEPER IS PROBABLY THE "DOVE-TAILED" HIVE, OR MOVABLE-FRAME HIVE. THE HIVE SHOULD HAVE EXTRACTING SUPERS RATHER THAN SECTION SUPERS WHICH ARE USED BY THE MORE EXPERIENCED APIARIST.

BESIDES THE HIVE, THE BEEKEEPER WILL NEED A BELLOWS SMOKER, A BEE VEIL WHICH CAN BE HOME-MADE UTILIZING ANY STIFF AND WIDE-BRIMMED HAT. TO THE BRIM OF THIS SEW A 5 OR 6 INCH STRIP OF BLACK SCREEN WIRE. TO THE BOTTOM OF THE SCREEN WIRE A STRIP OF CLOTH IS SEWN FOR TUCKING INTO YOUR COLLAR TO KEEP THE BEES OUT. YOU WILL ALSO NEED A SCRAPER OR WIDE CHISEL and FRUIT JARS FOR STORING THE HONEY.

BEES FOR THE HIVE MAY BE SECURED BY PURCHASING A SWARM FROM A NEARBY BEEKEEPER OR BY MAIL. (BEEKEEPING EQUIPMENT AND BEES ARE AVAILABLE THROUGH FARM-SUPPLY MAILORDER CATALOGS.)

YOU WILL ALSO NEED COMB FOUNDATIONS FOR STARTING GOOD STRAIGHT COMBS.

A BEEHIVE CAN BE PLACED IN ALMOST ANY SMALL CORNER FROM A COUNTRY GARDEN TO A CORNER OF A CITY BACKYARD, BUT THE BEES SHOULD BE PLACED IN AN AREA SO AS NOT TO DISTURB PEOPLE OR BE DISTURBED. THE HIVES SHOULD FACE EITHER THE SOUTH OR EAST and SHOULD BE AT LEAST 6 FEET APART.

UNTIL THE BEEKEEPER OBTAINS A LITTLE EXPERIENCE HE SHOULD REMOVE THE HONEY WITH AN EXTRACTOR or BY CUTTING THE HONEY AND COMB OUT, THEN REPLACING IT WITH A COMB STARTER.

ADDITIONAL INFORMATION ON THIS FUN HOBBY MAY BE OBTAINED FROM YOUR LOCAL LIBRARY OR BOOKSTORE. THERE ARE VERY INFORMATIVE BOOKS ON BEEKEEPING AVAILABLE FROM YOUR AGRICULTURAL EXTENSION OFFICE (COUNTY) OR AGRICULTURE SERVICE OFFICE.

Mark Gregory

Natural Crafts

GENTLENESS IS THE SECRET IN BEING A GOOD BEEKEEPER.

WHEN OPENING THE HIVE TO REMOVE THE HONEY-LADEN SUPERS, GO SLOWLY; DON'T OVER-SMOKE THE BEES. BE VERY CAREFUL NOT TO HARM OR IRRITATE THEM DURING HANDLING.

DON'T TRY TO WORK WITH BEES ON WINDY OR STORMY DAYS.

2

NATURAL
GARDENING
INDOORS
AND OUT

BECOME A NATURAL GARDENER AND PUT BACK MORE **INTO** THE LAND THAN YOU TAKE FROM IT.

NATURAL FOODS

MAKE *FRUIT LEATHER*, AN OLD-TIME CONFECTION THAT WILL REALLY GO FAST! PRUNES, APPLES, APRICOTS, EVEN PERSIMMONS ARE DELICIOUS PREPARED THIS WAY.

COVER A GALLON OF UNCOOKED FRUIT WITH WATER AND STEAM UNTIL SOFT. DRAIN OFF JUICE, PRESS THROUGH COLLANDER TO COLLECT REMAINING JUICE AND PULP. → *SHOULD BE AS THICK AS APPLE BUTTER* SWEETEN TO TASTE WITH HONEY and POUR ONTO OILED COOKIE SHEET. ALLOW TO DRY TO LEATHER CONSISTENCY (USUALLY REQUIRES 2 DAYS).

Getting started IN NATURAL GARDENING.

NATURAL GARDENING IS NOT ONLY FUN AND EASY TO DO, YOU CAN PRACTICE IT ANYWHERE -- ON YOUR PATIO WITH A POTTED PLANT OR WITH A THOUSAND ACRES. AND, YOU'RE HELPING TO PAY MANKIND'S DEBT TO THE GOOD EARTH.

TO BECOME A GOOD "NATURAL GARDENER" YOU MUST KNOW THE RULES. THEN YOU WILL DISCOVER THAT GARDENING IS FUN, RATHER THAN A CHORE, YOU WILL BE WORKING WITH THE GOOD EARTH, RATHER THAN FIGHTING IT.

1. USE NATURAL FERTILIZERS RATHER THAN ARTIFICIAL FERTILIZERS. SOME GOOD NATURAL FERTILIZERS ARE : *(AVAILABLE FROM GARDEN SUPPLY STORES)*
- Phosphate rock or granite dust
- Animal manures
- Minerals and, of course, Compost *(RECYCLED WASTE MATERIALS)*

2. DO NOT USE POISONS OR INSECTICIDES. INSTEAD, PLANT MORE HARDY PLANTS, OR MORE INSECT-RESISTANT PLANTS. TAKE THE TIME TO FIND OUT JUST WHAT PLANTS DO BEST IN YOUR PART OF THE COUNTRY. PULL WEEDS RATHER THAN SPRAY THEM WITH HERBICIDES. (YOU CAN USE THE DISCARDED WEEDS IN YOUR COMPOST PILE.)

3. LEARN TO USE MULCHES TO CONSERVE MOISTURE AND ADD MATERIALS NEEDED BY THE PLANTS TO THE SOIL.

NATURAL MULCHES
- OAK LEAVES
- PEAT MOSS
- DECAYED PINE NEEDLES
- CRUSHED LIMESTONE
- WOOD ASHES

4. USE COMPOST AND OTHER SOIL-BUILDING MATERIALS TO PUT LIFE-GIVING MATERIALS BACK INTO THE SOIL.

COMPOST PILE

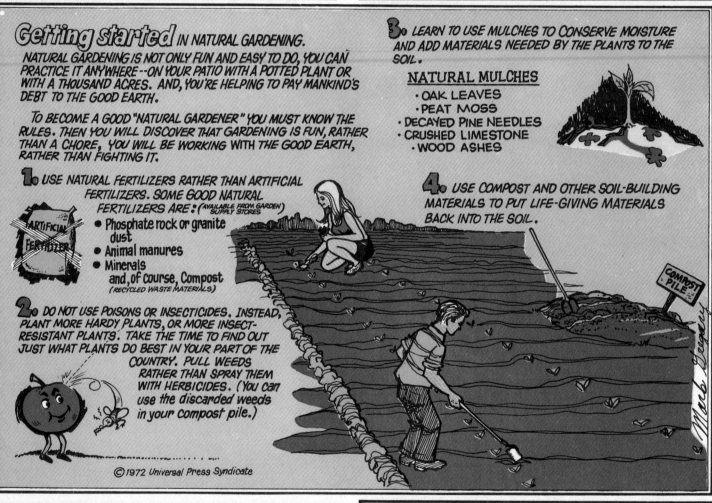

© 1972 Universal Press Syndicate

Natural Crafts

NOTHING BEATS **MANURE TEA** FOR GIVING SEEDLINGS A HEALTHY START. (GOOD FOR YOUR HOUSE-PLANTS AS WELL.)

MAKE A "PORCH-SIZE" TEA DRIPULATOR FROM A GALLON and A HALF-GALLON COFFEE CAN.

1. PUNCH SEVERAL HOLES IN THE CENTER OF THE BOTTOM OF THE LARGE CAN WITH A NAIL. FILL THE LARGER CAN WITH WELL-DRIED COW MANURE *(AVAILABLE FROM GARDEN CENTERS)* AND PLACE ATOP SMALLER CAN.

2. POUR ABOUT A QUART OF WATER INTO THE LARGE CAN, ALLOW IT TO SEEP THROUGH INTO THE SMALLER CAN. RESULTS SHOULD BE ABOUT THE COLOR OF TEA. A FEW DROPS ARE ADEQUATE FOR SEEDLINGS; A TSP. A MONTH FOR HOUSEPLANTS.

NATURAL FOODS

ANOTHER EXCELLENT NATURAL SEED STARTER IS EGG SHELLS. SAVE THE SHELLS FROM SOFT-BOILED EGGS AND PLANT FLOWER OR VEGETABLE SEEDS IN THEM.

IF YOU WANT TO PROVIDE AN EXTRA "BOOST" TO YOUR PLANTS, SOAK THE "STARTERS" IN "MANURE TEA" (A DILUTE SOLUTION OF WATER AND DRIED COW MANURE) BEFORE PLANTING SEEDS IN THEM.

IF YOU WANT TO GET YOUR GARDEN OFF TO A TRULY NATURAL START, TRY STARTING YOUR PLANTS IN HOME-MADE NATURAL SEED STARTERS.

SEED STARTERS CAN BE MADE FROM ANY LARGE, PITHY-CENTERED PLANT STALK SUCH AS CORN OR SUNFLOWER STALKS.

1. USING A HACKSAW OR SHARP KNIFE, CUT THE STALKS INTO 2-INCH LENGTHS.

2. USING A SHARP KNIFE, DIG OUT THE SOFT CENTER PITH LEAVING A LITTLE FOR A BOTTOM.

3. FILL THE "SEED-STARTERS" WITH A GOOD STARTING MIX SUCH AS WELL-COMPOSTED SOIL, OR "POTTING SOIL" AND PLACE IN A SHALLOW PAN.

4. PLANT SEEDS SUCH AS TOMATOES, PEPPERS, CABBAGE, FLOWERS, ETC. IN THEM AND WATER THEM WELL.

AFTER THE FIRST WATERING THE BEST WAY TO WATER IS TO POUR A LITTLE IN THE SHALLOW PAN AND ALLOW THE WATER TO SEEP UP THROUGH THE BOTTOM OF THE STARTERS.

5. PLACE THE STARTERS NEAR A WARM WINDOW OR IN A COLD FRAME.

6. AFTER THE LAST FROST THE PLANTS MAY BE PLACED IN THE GROUND, STARTER AND ALL. THE STARTER WILL EVENTUALLY DECAY FROM AROUND THE PLANT, BUT IT'S A GOOD IDEA TO POKE THE BOTTOM OUT OF THE STARTER BEFORE PLACING IT IN THE GROUND.

© 1973 UNIVERSAL PRESS SYNDICATE

Mark Gregory

Natural Crafts

A GOOD WAY OF RECYCLING OLD COFFEE CANS IS TO USE THEM AS MINIATURE GREENHOUSES OR "COLD-FRAMES."

1. CUT OUT BOTH ENDS.

2. PLACE PLASTIC LID ON THE TOP OF CAN.

3. POSITION CAN OVER PLANT.

START LOTS OF SEEDS -- Any you don't use will be welcomed by your friends and neighbors.

NATURAL FOODS

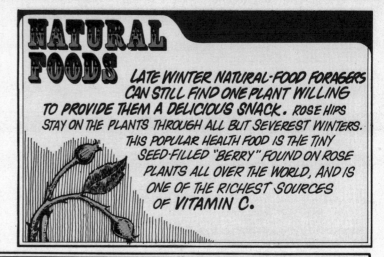

LATE WINTER NATURAL-FOOD FORAGERS CAN STILL FIND ONE PLANT WILLING TO PROVIDE THEM A DELICIOUS SNACK. ROSE HIPS STAY ON THE PLANTS THROUGH ALL BUT SEVEREST WINTERS. THIS POPULAR HEALTH FOOD IS THE TINY SEED-FILLED "BERRY" FOUND ON ROSE PLANTS ALL OVER THE WORLD, AND IS ONE OF THE RICHEST SOURCES OF VITAMIN C.

NOW IS THE TIME TO START YOUR **Natural Garden** INDOORS. WITH A LITTLE CARE AND EFFORT YOU'LL HAVE LOTS OF STURDY AND HEALTHY PLANTS READY FOR YOUR SPRING GARDEN.

1. THE FIRST REQUIREMENT FOR PROPERLY STARTING SEEDS INDOORS IS A SHALLOW BOX-LIKE CONTAINER TO PLANT THEM IN. THESE "BOXES" SHOULD HAVE NO BOTTOMS. PLACE THE BOXES IN PANS TO WATER THE SEEDS. POUR THE WATER INTO THE PANS AND ALLOW IT TO SEEP UP THROUGH THE FLATS FROM THE BOTTOM. WATERING FROM THE TOP DISTURBS THE TINY SEEDS, AND MAY CAUSE "DAMPING OFF" DISEASE AND LOSS OF THE PLANTS.

ONE OF THE BEST AND SIMPLEST SEED STARTING MIXTURES IS HALF POTTING SOIL (AVAILABLE FROM GARDEN SUPPLY CENTERS) AND HALF GOOD ORGANIC GARDEN SOIL. THE MIXTURE SHOULD BE LOOSE AND FAIRLY CRUMBLY.

2. WITH THE SEED FLATS PREPARED AND FILLED WITH THE CORRECT MIXTURE OF SOIL, THE NEXT STEP IS TO PLANT THE SEEDS. SPREAD THE SEEDS OUT EVENLY OVER THE TOP OF THE SOIL MIXTURE, THEN GENTLY PUSH INTO PLACE WITH A WOODEN MATCH STICK. PUSH THEM JUST UNDER THE SOIL - BUT DON'T COVER THEM UP.

3. FILL THE SHALLOW PANS WITH WATER AND KEEP DOING SO UNTIL YOU NOTICE WATER BEGINNING TO REACH THE SURFACE OF THE SOIL.

4. COVER EACH FLAT WITH A PIECE OF GLASS AND SET IT IN A WARM SUNNY SPOT SUCH AS A PATIO DOORWAY OR WINDOW. THE TEMPERATURE SHOULD BE FROM 65 to 75 DEGREES F.

5. WHEN THE SEEDS SPROUT, REMOVE THE GLASS AND MOVE THE FLATS TO A SUNNY BUT COOLER SPOT SUCH AS AN OUTDOOR SUNPORCH. DON'T WATER THEM TOO MUCH, BUT PROVIDE PLENTY OF AIR.

6. WHEN THE SEEDS HAVE ACQUIRED TWO SETS OF LEAVES, TRANSPLANT THEM INTO INDIVIDUAL CONTAINERS. WHEN THE WEATHER WARMS, PLANT THEM OUTDOORS.

Natural Crafts

EXCELLENT CONTAINERS FOR TRANSPLANTING INDOOR-STARTED SEEDS ARE "USED" PAPER DRINKING CUPS. RECYCLE THESE CUPS INTO SEED STARTERS BY PUNCHING SEVERAL HOLES IN THEIR BOTTOMS FOR WATER DRAINAGE. FILL WITH STARTING MIXTURE, AND TRANSPLANT INDIVIDUAL PLANTS INTO THEM. WHEN SETTING OUT THESE PLANTS OUTDOORS, MERELY TEAR OFF THE PAPER CUP.

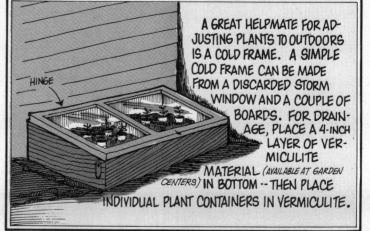

A GREAT HELPMATE FOR AD-JUSTING PLANTS TO OUTDOORS IS A COLD FRAME. A SIMPLE COLD FRAME CAN BE MADE FROM A DISCARDED STORM WINDOW AND A COUPLE OF BOARDS. FOR DRAIN-AGE, PLACE A 4-INCH LAYER OF VER-MICULITE MATERIAL (AVAILABLE AT GARDEN CENTERS) IN BOTTOM -- THEN PLACE INDIVIDUAL PLANT CONTAINERS IN VERMICULITE.

HINGE

START YOUR OWN "SEED BANK" and SAVE SEEDS EACH YEAR.

SURPLUS SEEDS CAN BE DRIED and SAVED FOR WINTER FEEDING OF BIRDS.

SAVE SEEDS FROM THIS YEAR'S FAVORITE PLANTS AND YOU'LL BE ABLE TO ENJOY THEM AGAIN NEXT YEAR. YOU WILL ALSO KNOW YOU'RE PRACTICING THE "NATURAL" WAY OF GARDENING.

SAVING SEEDS IS FUN AND EASY, AND YOU'LL SOON HAVE SO MANY SEEDS YOU WON'T HAVE ENOUGH FRIENDS AND NEIGHBORS TO GIVE THEM TO.

ONLY THE BEST OF YOUR VEGETABLES OR FLOWERS SHOULD BE SAVED FOR SEED -- THE SWEETEST, BIGGEST, ETC.

THE SEEDS OF VEGETABLES SUCH AS CORN, PEAS OR BEANS SHOULD BE ALLOWED TO DRY ON THE PLANT IF POSSIBLE.

SEEDS OF TOMATOES, CUCUMBER, SQUASH AND WATERMELON SHOULD BE LEFT ON THE PLANTS UNTIL THE FRUIT OR VEGETABLE IS SLIGHTLY OVERRIPE.

SEEDS OF FRUITS SHOULD BE SCRAPED OUT AND THEN SOAKED FOR A DAY IN WATER TO ALLOW THEM TO "FERMENT." THEY SHOULD BE WATCHED CAREFULLY AND NOT BE ALLOWED TO SPROUT. THE PULP AROUND THE SEEDS CAN THEN BE REMOVED EASILY BY RUBBING and THE SEEDS CAN BE DRIED ON PAPER.

ALL SEEDS SHOULD BE DRIED THOROUGHLY BEFORE STORAGE. THIS CAN BE DONE ON SHEETS OF PAPER IN A DRY, WARM, WELL-VENTILATED ROOM.

AFTER THE SEEDS ARE THOROUGHLY DRY THEY SHOULD BE PLACED IN PAPER ENVELOPES AND THE ENVELOPES THEN SHOULD BE PUT INTO GLASS JARS WITH LIDS. THE JARS SHOULD BE STORED IN A WARM, DRY ROOM.

IMPORTANT: SEEDS SHOULD BE TURNED OVER WHILE DRYING TO PREVENT FORMATION OF MOLD ON THEIR UNDERSIDES.

Mark Gregory

Natural Crafts

SEEDS FROM HYBRID PLANTS MAY REVERT BACK TO THE ORIGINAL PLANT IN A YEAR OR TWO, or THE SEEDS MAY NOT PRODUCE PLANTS.

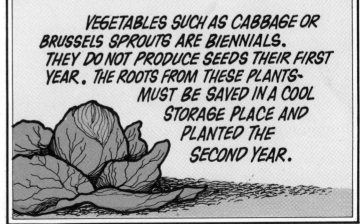

VEGETABLES SUCH AS CABBAGE OR BRUSSELS SPROUTS ARE BIENNIALS. THEY DO NOT PRODUCE SEEDS THEIR FIRST YEAR. THE ROOTS FROM THESE PLANTS MUST BE SAVED IN A COOL STORAGE PLACE AND PLANTED THE SECOND YEAR.

ALMOST ANY EDIBLE GRAIN or SEED WILL GROW EDIBLE SPROUTS, BUT THE MOST POPULAR ARE: SOYBEANS, MUNG BEANS, PEAS and EVEN WHEAT, OATS or BARLEY.

FOR A REAL TREAT, ADD SOYBEAN SPROUTS TO YOUR FAVORITE LETTUCE SALAD.

FOR A YEAR ROUND SUPPLY OF DELICIOUS FRESH FOOD TRY GROWING YOUR OWN SOYBEAN SPROUTS. IT'S FUN, EASY AND THE COST IS ONLY PENNIES. GROWING SPROUTS IS THE EASIEST TYPE OF GARDENING; THEY REQUIRE NO SOIL CULTIVATION, NO SUNLIGHT, NO DEMANDING ATTENTION, AND THEY'RE READY TO EAT WITHIN A FEW DAYS.

SOYBEANS CAN BE SPROUTED IN ALMOST ANY CONTAINER THAT HAS SOME SORT OF HOLES TO ALLOW FOR DRAINAGE. THE BEANS WILL SWELL TO OVER 6 TIMES THEIR ORIGINAL SIZE SO MAKE SURE THE CONTAINER IS LARGE ENOUGH.

SPROUTING BEANS IS SURPRISINGLY SIMPLE:

1. SOAK THE BEANS OVERNIGHT.

2. REMOVE FROM WATER, DRAIN, PLACE BEANS IN THE SPROUTING CONTAINER. PLACE IN A WARM, DARK SPOT.

3. POUR LUKEWARM WATER OVER THE BEANS AT LEAST 5 OR 6 TIMES A DAY, MAKING SURE YOU FLUSH THEM THOROUGHLY, BUT DRAIN WELL.

4. IN 3 TO 6 DAYS THE BEANS WILL HAVE GROWN DELICIOUS SPROUTS.

5. SPROUTS ARE FRESH VEGETABLES SO KEEP IN A COOL PLACE.

SOYBEAN SPROUTS ARE DELICIOUS AS IS, OR ADDED TO SALADS, SOUPS, STEWS AND EVEN BREADS. THEY ARE VERY FRAGILE SO DON'T ADD THEM INTO HOT FOODS UNTIL THE VERY LAST MINUTE.

SOYBEANS FOR SPROUTING ARE AVAILABLE AT NATURAL FOODS STORES AS WELL AS SOME GARDEN CENTERS. MAKE SURE YOU BUY THIS YEAR'S CROP, AND USE ONLY SOUND, WHOLE, FRESH BEANS MEANT FOR HUMAN CONSUMPTION. PICK OUT ALL THE CHAFF AND BAD-LOOKING BEANS.

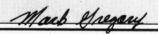

Mark Gregory

Natural Crafts

ONE OF THE BEST SPROUTING CONTAINERS IS A LARGE-MOUTHED FRUIT JAR FIXED UP A LITTLE SPECIAL.

1. CUT A PIECE OF NEW CLEAN SCREENWIRE TO FIT OVER THE MOUTH OF THE JAR.

2. HOLD THE SCREENWIRE IN PLACE WITH AN ORDINARY CANNING RING-LID HOLDER.

3. SPROUTS IN THIS CONTAINER MAY EASILY BE FLUSHED AND DRAINED.

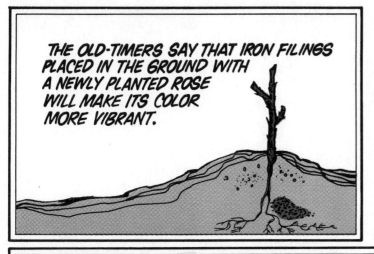

THE OLD-TIMERS SAY THAT IRON FILINGS PLACED IN THE GROUND WITH A NEWLY PLANTED ROSE WILL MAKE ITS COLOR MORE VIBRANT.

NATURAL FOODS

A ROSE GLAZE MAY EVEN BE USED ON SOME MEATS and CONSISTS OF ROSE-WATER, MELTED BUTTER AND HONEY.

EVERY EARLY FARM HOMESTEAD HAD LOTS OF ROSES GROWING AROUND IT, AND THEY NOT ONLY LOOKED PRETTY AND SMELLED NICE, THEY WERE USED TO MAKE A VARIETY OF THINGS FROM FOODS TO TOILETRIES.

ONE OF THE FAVORITES OF THE OLD-TIMERS WAS "ROSE-PETAL" JAM.

1. GATHER ONE CUP OF FRESHLY-OPENED ROSE PETALS. CAREFULLY SNIP OFF THE WHITE BASES OF THE PETALS. (THESE ARE BITTER.)

2. PLACE THE PETALS IN A BLENDER WITH A CUP OF WATER AND THE JUICE OF ONE LEMON. BLEND, ADDING 2 CUPS OF HONEY.

WARNING
DO NOT USE PLANTS THAT HAVE BEEN SPRAYED WITH INSECTICIDE

© 1973 UNIVERSAL PRESS SYNDICATE

3. POUR A PACKAGE OF PECTIN INTO 3/4 CUP OF WATER. BRING THIS TO A BOIL, THEN BOIL HARD FOR ONE MINUTE, STIRRING CONSTANTLY.

4. POUR THE PECTIN INTO THE BLENDER WITH THE ROSE-HONEY MIXTURE AND BLEND INGREDIENTS THOROUGHLY.

5. POUR INTO SMALL JELLY JARS AND SEAL.

6. THIS JELLY MUST BE FROZEN OR REFRIGERATED.

A FAVORITE SUMMERTIME TREAT IS ROSE FRITTERS.

MAKE A BATTER OF 1 CUP FLOUR, 1 TEASPOON BAKING POWDER, 2 TABLESPOONS HONEY, 1/2 TEASPOON SALT AND 2 EGGS. WHEN MIXED GENTLY, STIR IN 1 CUP OF FRESH ROSE PETALS. DROP BY SPOONFULS INTO HOT FAT (360°). DRAIN AND DRIZZLE WITH WARM HONEY.

ROSE-WATER IS ANOTHER OLD-FASHIONED ROSE PRODUCT CHERISHED BY YOUR GRANDMOTHER. MERELY PLACE ROSE PETALS IN WATER AND BRING TO A BOIL, THEN SIMMER. THIS SWEET-SMELLING WATER WAS ADDED TO THE BATH.

Natural Crafts

ONE OLD-FASHIONED GIFT WAS LITTLE BAGS OF ROSE PETALS WHICH COULD ADD A BIT OF FRAGRANCE TO THE LINEN CHEST.

1. GATHER FRESHLY OPENED PETALS AND DRY THEM ON A WARM WINDOW SILL.

2. ADD A FEW BITS OF MINT LEAVES AND A LITTLE GROUND CINNAMON, ALLSPICE and GINGER.

3. PLACE ALL IN A SMALL OPEN-MESH BAG AND TIE WITH A BRIGHT RIBBON.

HERBS ARE A NATURAL INSECT REPELLENT AND ARE IMMUNE TO MOST PLANT DISEASES.
PLANT HERBS AMONG YOUR VEGETABLES THIS SUMMER AND ENJOY A BUG-FREE GARDEN

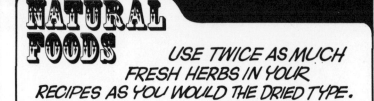

NATURAL FOODS

USE TWICE AS MUCH FRESH HERBS IN YOUR RECIPES AS YOU WOULD THE DRIED TYPE.

HERBS HAVE BEEN VALUED FOR HUNDREDS OF MEDICINAL PURPOSES SINCE AROUND 3,000 B.C.!

Grow A Winter Herb Garden

...AND ENJOY THE FRAGRANCE AND CULINARY DELIGHTS OF YOUR FAVORITE HERBS YEAR ROUND.

Note: The herbs pictured here grow best INSIDE the house any time of year.

Winter Herbs

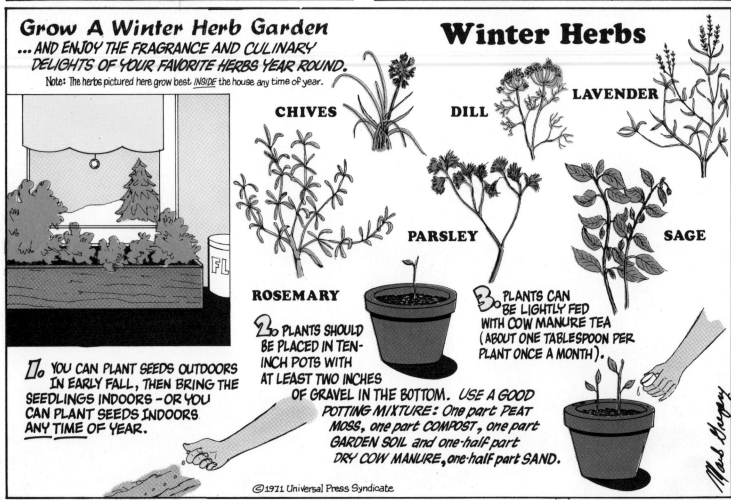

CHIVES

DILL

LAVENDER

PARSLEY

SAGE

ROSEMARY

1. YOU CAN PLANT SEEDS OUTDOORS IN EARLY FALL, THEN BRING THE SEEDLINGS INDOORS – OR YOU CAN PLANT SEEDS INDOORS ANY TIME OF YEAR.

2. PLANTS SHOULD BE PLACED IN TEN-INCH POTS WITH AT LEAST TWO INCHES OF GRAVEL IN THE BOTTOM. USE A GOOD POTTING MIXTURE: One part PEAT MOSS, one part COMPOST, one part GARDEN SOIL and one-half part DRY COW MANURE, one-half part SAND.

3. PLANTS CAN BE LIGHTLY FED WITH COW MANURE TEA (ABOUT ONE TABLESPOON PER PLANT ONCE A MONTH).

©1971 Universal Press Syndicate

Natural Crafts

MAKE WINDOW PLANTING BOXES TO HOLD YOUR HERBS – EACH BOX WILL HOLD 3 POTTED HERBS ... OR YOU CAN PLANT DIRECTLY IN THE BOXES (IF YOU INCLUDE A DRAINAGE PAN IN THE BOXES).

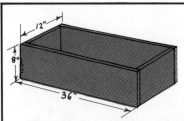

1. USE CEDAR BOARDS 8"x 12"x 36" or 48" IN CONSTRUCTING BOXES.

2. PLACE TWO INCHES OF GRAVEL IN BOTTOM. PLACE POTS ON TOP WITH SPHAGNUM MOSS AROUND POTS.

BECAUSE OF ITS ASTRINGENT QUALITIES PLANTAIN LEAVES WERE USED BY THE "MOUNTAIN PEOPLE" AS A "POULTICE" FOR CUTS AND SCRATCHES.

A SOMEWHAT BITTER TEA WAS OFTEN MADE FROM PLANTAIN LEAVES. A HANDFUL OF LEAVES WERE DROPPED INTO BOILING WATER AND ALLOWED TO STEEP UNTIL THE DESIRED TASTE WAS REACHED.

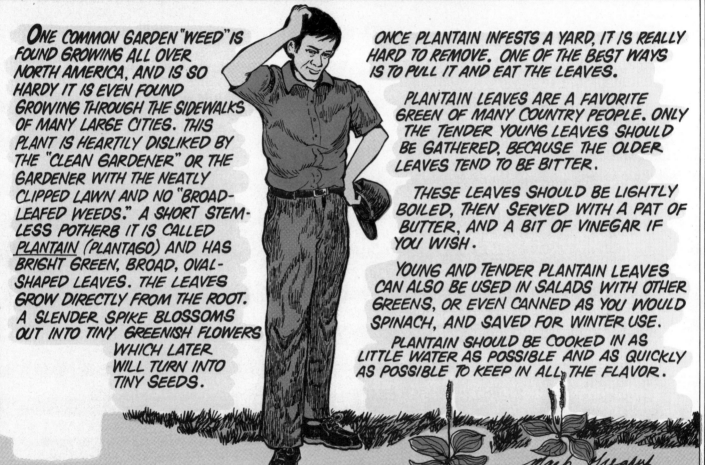

ONE COMMON GARDEN "WEED" IS FOUND GROWING ALL OVER NORTH AMERICA, AND IS SO HARDY IT IS EVEN FOUND GROWING THROUGH THE SIDEWALKS OF MANY LARGE CITIES. THIS PLANT IS HEARTILY DISLIKED BY THE "CLEAN GARDENER" OR THE GARDENER WITH THE NEATLY CLIPPED LAWN AND NO "BROAD-LEAFED WEEDS." A SHORT STEM-LESS POTHERB IT IS CALLED PLANTAIN (PLANTAGO) AND HAS BRIGHT GREEN, BROAD, OVAL-SHAPED LEAVES. THE LEAVES GROW DIRECTLY FROM THE ROOT. A SLENDER SPIKE BLOSSOMS OUT INTO TINY GREENISH FLOWERS WHICH LATER WILL TURN INTO TINY SEEDS.

© 1973 UNIVERSAL PRESS SYNDICATE

ONCE PLANTAIN INFESTS A YARD, IT IS REALLY HARD TO REMOVE. ONE OF THE BEST WAYS IS TO PULL IT AND EAT THE LEAVES.

PLANTAIN LEAVES ARE A FAVORITE GREEN OF MANY COUNTRY PEOPLE. ONLY THE TENDER YOUNG LEAVES SHOULD BE GATHERED, BECAUSE THE OLDER LEAVES TEND TO BE BITTER.

THESE LEAVES SHOULD BE LIGHTLY BOILED, THEN SERVED WITH A PAT OF BUTTER, AND A BIT OF VINEGAR IF YOU WISH.

YOUNG AND TENDER PLANTAIN LEAVES CAN ALSO BE USED IN SALADS WITH OTHER GREENS, OR EVEN CANNED AS YOU WOULD SPINACH, AND SAVED FOR WINTER USE.

PLANTAIN SHOULD BE COOKED IN AS LITTLE WATER AS POSSIBLE AND AS QUICKLY AS POSSIBLE TO KEEP IN ALL THE FLAVOR.

Natural Crafts

DON'T MOW YOUR YARD QUITE SO OFTEN. ALLOW SOME OF THE WILD WEEDS AND FLOWERS TO GROW AND LEARN TO IDENTIFY AND ENJOY THEM.

MAKE YOUR YARD A "MINI" PARK YOU AND YOUR FAMILY CAN ENJOY, WITH A LARGE NUMBER OF PLANTS, NOT JUST A CLIPPED AND MANICURED "GREEN CARPET."

OTHER NATURAL GARDEN PREDATORS WHICH KEEP INSECT PESTS UNDER CONTROL ARE TOADS, FROGS, BIRDS, BATS AND SNAKES.

COMBATING INSECT PESTS WITH NATURAL INSECT PREDATORS RATHER THAN PESTICIDES LEAVES YOU FREE FROM THE WORRY OF WHETHER THE PESTICIDE IS WASHED COMPLETELY OFF YOUR PRODUCE.

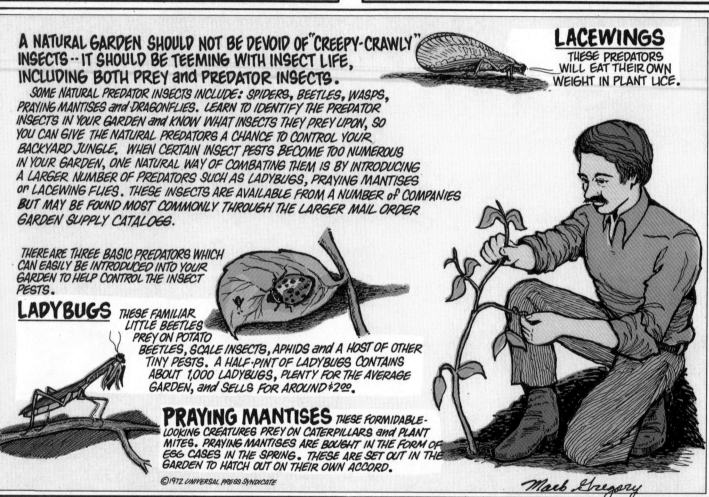

A NATURAL GARDEN SHOULD NOT BE DEVOID OF "CREEPY-CRAWLY" INSECTS -- IT SHOULD BE TEEMING WITH INSECT LIFE, INCLUDING BOTH PREY AND PREDATOR INSECTS.

SOME NATURAL PREDATOR INSECTS INCLUDE: SPIDERS, BEETLES, WASPS, PRAYING MANTISES AND DRAGONFLIES. LEARN TO IDENTIFY THE PREDATOR INSECTS IN YOUR GARDEN AND KNOW WHAT INSECTS THEY PREY UPON, SO YOU CAN GIVE THE NATURAL PREDATORS A CHANCE TO CONTROL YOUR BACKYARD JUNGLE. WHEN CERTAIN INSECT PESTS BECOME TOO NUMEROUS IN YOUR GARDEN, ONE NATURAL WAY OF COMBATING THEM IS BY INTRODUCING A LARGER NUMBER OF PREDATORS SUCH AS LADYBUGS, PRAYING MANTISES OR LACEWING FLIES. THESE INSECTS ARE AVAILABLE FROM A NUMBER OF COMPANIES BUT MAY BE FOUND MOST COMMONLY THROUGH THE LARGER MAIL ORDER GARDEN SUPPLY CATALOGS.

THERE ARE THREE BASIC PREDATORS WHICH CAN EASILY BE INTRODUCED INTO YOUR GARDEN TO HELP CONTROL THE INSECT PESTS.

LACEWINGS
THESE PREDATORS WILL EAT THEIR OWN WEIGHT IN PLANT LICE.

LADYBUGS
THESE FAMILIAR LITTLE BEETLES PREY ON POTATO BEETLES, SCALE INSECTS, APHIDS AND A HOST OF OTHER TINY PESTS. A HALF-PINT OF LADYBUGS CONTAINS ABOUT 1,000 LADYBUGS, PLENTY FOR THE AVERAGE GARDEN, AND SELLS FOR AROUND $2.00.

PRAYING MANTISES
THESE FORMIDABLE-LOOKING CREATURES PREY ON CATERPILLARS AND PLANT MITES. PRAYING MANTISES ARE BOUGHT IN THE FORM OF EGG CASES IN THE SPRING. THESE ARE SET OUT IN THE GARDEN TO HATCH OUT ON THEIR OWN ACCORD.

© 1972 UNIVERSAL PRESS SYNDICATE

Mack Gregory

Natural Crafts

OF COURSE, THE EASIEST, BUT NOW-A-DAYS SEEMINGLY FORGOTTEN WAY OF CONTROLLING INSECT PESTS IS PICKING THEM OFF BY HAND.

MANY FARM YOUNGSTERS HAVE MADE A SUMMER "SALARY" PICKING THOSE FEROCIOUS-LOOKING GREEN "TOMATO WORMS" OFF MOM'S TOMATO PLANTS.

MAKE FRIENDS WITH YOUR NEIGHBORS... COLLECT THEIR "BAGGED" LEAVES AND GRASS CLIPPINGS FOR YOUR COMPOST PILE.

START YOUR MORNING OFF WITH A GOOD HEARTY NATURAL MEAL LIKE GRANDMOTHER DID. HAVE CORN MEAL MUSH, FRIED AND SERVED WITH PLENTY OF BUTTER and HONEY. *TO MAKE MUSH CAKES:* ADD 2 CUPS OF CORN MEAL (MIXED WITH ONE PINT OF COLD WATER) TO 2½ PINTS OF BOILING WATER AND A TABLESPOON OF SALT. POUR INTO SQUARE CAKE PANS, ALLOW TO COOL AND HARDEN, THEN SLICE AND FRY.

COMPOSTING

COMPOSTING IS THE SECRET OF A GOOD NATURAL GARDENER. COMPOST IS THE ONE INGREDIENT THAT CAN DO MORE TOWARD BUILDING YOUR SOIL THAN ANY OTHER. MAKING COMPOST IS EASY--AND A GREAT WAY OF DISPOSING OF MANY UNWANTED WASTE MATERIALS. *It's never too late to start collecting!*

PRACTICALLY ANYTHING CAN GO INTO YOUR COMPOST, FROM COOKING SCRAPS TO GRASS CLIPPINGS and LEAVES.

BACKYARD GARDENERS CAN MAKE COMPOST USING NOTHING MORE THAN A LARGE GARBAGE CAN. FILL WITH LEAVES, GRASS, DEAD VEGETABLE PLANTS, KITCHEN SCRAPS, ETC. ABOUT EVERY 6 INCHES, ADD A 3 INCH LAYER OF DRIED MANURE (AVAILABLE AT GARDEN SUPPLY CENTERS), THEN A 3 INCH LAYER OF GARDEN SOIL.

DAMPEN EACH LAYER SLIGHTLY, PLACE LID ON CAN AND LEAVE FOR A MONTH. EVERY FOUR OR FIVE DAYS STIR THE MATERIALS TO KEEP THEM FROM COMPACTING. KEEP MOIST, BUT NOT SOAKED.

YOUR COMPOSTING CAN ALSO BE DONE ON A LARGER SCALE BY BUILDING A COMPOST PIT OR PILE. THE SIZE OF YOUR COMPOST PIT CAN BE ALMOST ANYTHING YOU FEEL YOU CAN FILL. HOWEVER, IT SHOULD NOT BE OVER 4 OR 5 FEET IN HEIGHT. NAIL UP A GIANT, THREE-SIDED BOX WITH A SIDE OPEN FOR EASY ACCESS TO THE MATERIALS. "LAYER" YOUR DISPOSABLE MATERIALS IN THIS BOX.

A TYPICAL COMPOST MIGHT BE MADE UP OF THIS ➔
- LAYER of TWIGS, BRANCHES
- LAYER of LEAVES, GRASS
- LAYER of DRIED MANURE
- LAYER of LEAVES, GRASS
- LAYER of GARDEN SOIL
- LAYER of WOOD ASHES

CONTINUE LAYERING UNTIL YOU FILL THE PIT. SOAK THE PIT THOROUGHLY WITH WATER–COVER WITH A TOP LAYER OF SOIL. TURN PILE WEEKLY–SHOULD BE READY IN 3 OR 4 WEEKS.

TO BREAK DOWN READILY, MATERIALS USED IN COMPOSTING MUST BE AS SMALL AS YOU CAN SHRED THEM. YOU CAN USE A POWER SHREDDER TO SHRED LEAVES, BRANCHES, EVEN BONES.

A SLOWER PROCESS FOR SMALLER COMPOSTING IS A "MACHETE" AND A LARGE CHOPPING BLOCK.

YOU CAN SHRED LEAVES BY DRIVING YOUR LAWN MOWER OVER THEM. THE MOWER SHOULD BE EQUIPPED WITH A CATCHING BAG. YOU MAY HAVE TO EMPTY THE BAG AND RUN OVER THE LEAVES SEVERAL TIMES TO GET THEM FINE ENOUGH FOR GOOD COMPOSTING.

THE EARTHWORMS IN AN AVERAGE ACRE OF GOOD FERTILE SOIL WILL CONSUME, DIGEST and "REVITALIZE" OVER 15 TONS OF EARTH IN A YEAR'S TIME.

MUNCH MUNCH

NATURAL FOODS

GATHER A CUPFUL OF WILD MUSTARD SEEDS. SPREAD OUT ON PAPER TOWELING TO DRY, THEN STORE IN HERB BOTTLES. USE THEM TO REALLY SPICE UP SALADS, BARBECUE SAUCES AND PICKLES.

Raising Earthworms

IS A PROJECT THE ENTIRE FAMILY WILL ENJOY, AND CAN PROVIDE NOT ONLY LOTS OF "FISHIN' BAIT," BUT ALSO THE RICHEST COMPOST POSSIBLE FOR FLOWERS and VEGETABLES. RAISING EARTHWORMS IS ALSO A FUN and EASY MONEY MAKING VENTURE FOR THE YOUNGSTERS.

EARTHWORMS THRIVE IN TEMPERATURES RANGING FROM 60° TO 70°, SO IT'S BEST TO START THE "WORM FARM" IN THE SPRING. ALMOST ANY CONTAINER WILL DO, BUT ONE OF THE BEST IS A DISCARDED No. 3 WASH OR LAUNDRY TUB. IF PROPERLY "MANAGED" A "FARM" OF THIS SIZE CAN PRODUCE OVER **3,000** WORMS PER YEAR.

1 CUT A DRAIN HOLE IN THE BOTTOM OF THE TUB, THEN COVER THE BOTTOM WITH A PIECE OF SCREEN WIRE.

2 PLACE A LAYER OF LEAVES IN THE BOTTOM OF THE TUB.

3 MAKE A BEDDING MIXTURE OF 1/3 PART WELL-DRIED COW MANURE AND 1/3 PART PEAT MOSS (AVAILABLE AT GARDEN SUPPLY CENTERS) AND 1/3 PART GARDEN SOIL. MIX IN 1 POUND OF CORNMEAL, THEN FILL TUB WITH THIS MIXTURE.

4 PLACE ABOUT 200 EARTHWORMS IN THE TUB (EARTHWORMS ARE AVAILABLE FROM BAIT DEALERS.)

5 COVER TUB WITH BURLAP SACK AND ADD WATER UNTIL SOIL IS MOIST -- BUT NOT "SOGGY." (FOR GOOD RESULTS, THE FARM SHOULD BE KEPT MOIST.)

6 PLACE IN A PROTECTED SHADY AREA.

7 FEED THE WORMS AT LEAST ONCE A WEEK. EARTHWORM FOOD CAN BE ALMOST ANY ORGANIC SUBSTANCE THAT BREAKS DOWN EASILY -- TABLE SCRAPS, COFFEE GROUNDS, CORNMEAL, KITCHEN FAT (USED SPARINGLY), DISCARDED VEGETABLE LEAVES, ETC.

8 TO HARVEST WORMS REMOVE HANDFULS OF THE BEDDING WHICH NOW HAS BEEN CONVERTED TO "COMPOST" AND PLACE ON A FLAT BOARD. ALLOW WORMS TO CONGREGATE AT BOTTOM OF PILE, THEN RAKE OFF TOP. LEAVE A FEW WORMS IN TUB AS "BROOD STOCK."

9 THE WORM BEDDING CAN BE REPLACED ABOUT ONCE A MONTH, AND THE WORM-ENRICHED BEDDING, WHEN ADDED TO VEGETABLE AND FLOWER GARDENS, WILL GIVE YOUR PLANTS A REVITALIZING BOOST.

© 1972
Universal Press Syndicate

Marb Gregory

Natural Crafts

A SIMPLE "WORM HATCHERY" FOR RAISING EARTHWORMS CAN BE BUILT INDOORS IN A CELLAR, BASEMENT or GARAGE.

WORM FARM

CONSTRUCT A STACK OF BOXES AS SHOWN. EACH BOX MUST HAVE A DRAINAGE HOLE COVERED WITH SCREEN WIRE, AND SHOULD BE SEPARATED FROM THE OTHER BOXES WITH SPACERS TO ALLOW AIR TO CIRCULATE.

3
COOKING

AND FOOD
PREPARATION

IF YOU COOK IN FOIL WRAP, DON'T BURY IT, OR LEAVE IT WHERE WILD ANIMALS CAN GET IT.

THEY EAT THE FOOD-COVERED FOIL, AND IT REMAINS IN THEIR STOMACH TO CAUSE A PAINFUL DEATH.

NATURAL FOODS

TRY THIS FOR A GREAT BARBECUE SAUCE:

- 1 CUP TOMATO JUICE
- ½ CUP BROWN SUGAR
- ½ CUP RED WINE
- ½ TEASPOON DRY MUSTARD
- ½ TEASPOON SALT
- ½ TEASPOON CAYENNE PEPPER
- CRUSHED GARLIC and ONION
- BAY LEAVES

HEAT SLOWLY OVER LOW FLAME, STIRRING UNTIL ALL INGREDIENTS ARE MIXED.

IF YOU WANT A TASTE OF REAL "BARBECUE," TRY AN AUTHENTIC WESTERN STYLE "PIT-BARBECUE." THE GRANDDADDY OF ALL BARBECUING, THIS OLD-TIME WAY OF COOKING WAS USED TO FEED HUNGRY COW-HANDS WHILE ON THE TRAIL, AND TODAY CAN PROVIDE A "BARBECUE" YOUR ENTIRE NEIGHBORHOOD CAN ENJOY.

Barbecue Sauce

- 10 OR 12 TOMATOES
- 1 PINT COLD WATER
- 1 CUP BROWN SUGAR
- 1 TABLESPOON SALT
- 1 CUP CIDER VINEGAR
- 2 CLOVES GARLIC
- 2 BAY LEAVES
- 1 LARGE MINCED ONION
- 1 LEMON
- 1 TABLESPOON CHILI POWDER
- 1 TEASPOON POWDERED OREGANO
- 1 TEASPOON BLACK PEPPER
- 2 TEASPOONS DRY MUSTARD

SIMMER OVER LOW HEAT, STIRRING TO PREVENT STICKING. SIMMER 30 TO 40 MINUTES.

IT WILL TAKE A BIT OF SPACE, BECAUSE YOU'LL NEED TO DIG A PIT 4 FEET WIDE, 6 FEET LONG and 4 FEET DEEP. THIS SIZE PIT WILL COOK A SIDE OF PORK, SEVERAL HAMS or A SMALL SIDE OF BEEF.

1. THE FIRST STEP IS TO DIG THE PIT. IT SHOULD BE DUG IN A CLAY TYPE OF SOIL RATHER THAN A SANDY SOIL.

2. BUILD A FIRE IN THE BOTTOM OF THE PIT. IT SHOULD BE OF OAK, HICKORY OR SOME OTHER HARDWOOD. KEEP ADDING TO THE FIRE UNTIL YOU HAVE BUILT A BED OF COALS ABOUT A FOOT DEEP IN THE PIT.

3. WHOLE HAMS OR BEEF CUT INTO 15 OR 20 POUND CHUNKS MAKE EXCELLENT MEATS FOR PIT BARBECUING -- COVER THE MEAT LIBERALLY WITH A GOOD BARBECUE SAUCE AND WRAP IN BUTCHER PAPER.

4. WRAP THE PAPER-COVERED MEAT IN WET BURLAP SACKS AND TIE WITH WIRE.

5. PLACE THE BURLAP AND PAPER WRAPPED CHUNKS OF MEAT ON THE RED HOT COALS.

6. COVER THE PIT WITH A PIECE OF SHEET METAL LARGE ENOUGH TO COVER IT COMPLETELY.

7. SHOVEL THE DIRT BACK OVER SHEET METAL MAKING SURE ALL EDGES ARE COVERED.

8. LEAVE THE BARBECUE ALONE. WHEN COOKING HAMS OR A SIDE OF BEEF IT SHOULD BE LEFT 16 TO 18 HOURS. SMALLER MEAT CUTS MAY REQUIRE ONLY 12 TO 14 HOURS.

9. REMOVE THE MEAT, SWAB WITH MORE SAUCE, CARVE and SERVE.

Natural Crafts

A TOY WATER PISTOL FILLED WITH WATER AND A PINCH OF BAKING SODA MAKES A GREAT FIRE EXTINGUISHER FOR FLARE-UPS WHEN COOKING OVER AN OUTDOOR FIRE.

ROAST POTATOES AND SIMILAR FOODS WRAPPED IN SEVERAL LAYERS OF WET NEWSPAPER RATHER THAN FOIL. THEN BURN THE PAPER.

NATURAL FUELS ARE A PRECIOUS AND NONRENEWABLE COMMODITY WE CANNOT AFFORD TO WASTE.

THE CHINESE WOK IS AS EASILY USED FOR OUTDOOR COOKING AS INDOORS, AND THE RESULTS CAN BE DELICIOUS. IF YOUR **WOK** ISN'T EQUIPPED WITH AN ADAPTER RING, MERELY PILE ROCKS IN A CIRCLE TO SUPPORT IT AND BUILD A SMALL BED OF HOT COALS IN THE CIRCLE.

ONE OF THE MOST NATURAL STYLES OF FOOD PREPARATION IS **CHINESE COOKING.** EXTREMELY EFFICIENT and ECONOMICAL, IT REQUIRES LITTLE FUEL TO PREPARE AN EXTREMELY HEALTHFUL AND SUCCULENT MEAL.

THE SECRET IN THE LIGHT DELICIOUS TASTE OF CHINESE COOKING IS IN PROPER PREPARATION OF THE FOODS *BEFORE* COOKING, THEN A *HIGH HEAT* TO COOK THE MATERIALS QUICKLY, RETAINING ALL THE NUTRITION AND TEXTURE -- AS WELL AS FLAVOR and FRAGRANCE -- OF THE FOODS.

THE EASIEST TRADITIONAL MANNER OF COOKING TO LEARN IS THAT OF *QUICK STIR-FRYING* USING THE CHINESE "WOK"-A LARGE SAUCER-SHAPED METAL PAN WITH HANDLES ON EACH END. IN USING THIS VESSEL, IT IS FIRST HEATED, THEN A SMALL AMOUNT OF COOKING OIL HEATED IN IT. FINALLY THE PREPARED MEATS and/or VEGETABLES ARE PLACED IN THE HOT OIL AND COOKED ALMOST IMMEDIATELY. COOKING USUALLY REQUIRES FROM 3 to 6 MINUTES.

THE SECRET IN THIS FAST COOKING IS IN THE SHAPE OF THE WOK, PLUS THE PREPARATION OF THE FOODS BEFORE COOKING. THEY MUST BE CUT UP INTO TINY PIECES SO THEY WILL COOK ALMOST IMMEDIATELY.

FOR THIS YOU WILL NEED A GOOD WOODEN CHOPPING BLOCK AND A LARGE CLEAVER, KEPT RAZOR SHARP. BECAUSE OF THE QUICK-NESS WITH WHICH THE WOK COOKS, YOU'LL NEED ALL YOUR MATERIALS AND INGREDIENTS, PROPERLY MIXED, MEASURED AND DICED OR CUT UP, BEFORE STARTING TO HEAT THE OIL.

Mark Gregory

Natural Crafts

THE WOK MUST BE PROPERLY BROKEN IN AND CARED FOR IF IT IS TO GIVE YOU LONG AND GOOD SERVICE.

TO BREAK IN A NEW WOK HEAT IT ON THE STOVE AND RUB IN A GOOD NATURAL VEGETABLE OIL SUCH AS PEANUT OIL. WIPE OFF THE EXCESS WITH A CLEAN CLOTH WHILE THE WOK IS STILL HOT.

TO CLEAN THE WOK AFTER COOKING, RINSE UNDER HOT WATER, THEN REHEAT IT WITH FRESH VEGETABLE OIL, AGAIN WIPING OFF EXCESS WITH A CLEAN CLOTH.

UNCOMPLICATE YOUR LIFE. LEARN TO LIVE WITH THE SIMPLEST OF DEVICES.

DUTCH OVEN
CAMP BREAD

BANNOCK OR "CAMP BREAD" CAN EASILY BE COOKED IN A DUTCH OVEN. MIX FOUR CUPS FLOUR, 6 TABLESPOONS SUGAR, 1 TEASPOON SALT, 4 TEASPOONS BAKING POWDER, THEN ADD 1/3 CUP WATER OR MILK. PRESS INTO DUTCH OVEN AND BAKE FOR ABOUT 15 MINUTES FOR EACH 1-INCH THICKNESS.

"DUTCH OVEN COOKING" IS THE TRADITIONAL COOKING METHOD OF THE EARLY OUTDOORSMAN. THIS EXTREMELY VERSATILE METHOD IS THE GRANDDADDY OF "ONE-POT COOKING." WITH A LITTLE PRACTICE A CAMP COOK CAN PROVIDE A HEARTY GAME STEW OR A MOUTH-WATERING BATCH OF BISCUITS FROM THIS PRACTICAL POT.

AN AUTHENTIC DUTCH OVEN IS ACTUALLY A CAST IRON POT. IT HAS THREE SHORT LEGS AND, SOMETIMES, A HANDLE. A TIGHT FITTING CAST IRON LID IS MADE TO FIT DOWN INTO A RIM AROUND THE OUTSIDE EDGE OF THE POT. THE LID IS DOMED AND HAS A LIFTING RING IN ITS CENTER. THESE TWO PIECES CAN NOT ONLY BE USED AS AN OVEN, THE POT CAN SERVE AS A FRYING PAN and THE LID AS A GRIDDLE.

THERE ARE TWO BASIC COOKING METHODS WITH DUTCH OVENS : BELOW GROUND and ABOVE GROUND.

© 1972 Universal Press Syndicate

UNDERGROUND : THIS METHOD WORKS FOR STEWS, ROASTS, BIRDS, BEANS, ETC. DIG A PIT 2×2×2 FEET DEEP AND COVER THE BOTTOM OF THE PIT WITH RED HOT COALS. PLACE THE DUTCH OVEN, FILLED WITH IN-GREDIENTS, INTO THE PIT. PLACE THE LID ON THE OVEN AND PACK A LAYER OF COALS ALL AROUND THE OVEN AND OVER ITS TOP. COVER THIS WITH AT LEAST 6 INCHES OF DIRT. (MAKE SURE THERE ARE NO FLAMMABLE MATERIALS, SUCH AS LEAVES, IN THE SOIL.) AFTER A DAY OF HIKING, HUNTING OR FISHING YOU RETURN TO CAMP TO A HOT MEAL.

ABOVE GROUND :
THIS METHOD IS USED TO BAKE BREAD, PIES, BISCUITS, ETC. PREHEAT THE OVEN ON A GOOD PILE OF HOT COALS. REMOVE THE OVEN FROM THE COALS, COAT THE INSIDE WITH GREASE AND PLACE THE DOUGH IN THE OVEN. MOVE THE OVEN BACK ONTO THE COALS, COVER WITH THE LID, THEN SCOOP HOT COALS ONTO THE LID. THE EDGE OF THE LID IS SHAPED TO HOLD THE COALS IN PLACE. FOR GOLDEN BROWN BREAD AND BISCUITS, YOU WILL HAVE TO KEEP ADDING COALS TO THE LID UNTIL THE BREAD IS DONE.

Mark Klagman

Natural Crafts

DUTCH OVENS MUST BE SEASONED CAREFULLY WHEN FIRST PURCHASED. TO SEASON, COAT THE INSIDE OF THE POT WITH BACON FAT, THEN KEEP IT SMOKING HOT FOR TWO HOURS, APPLYING THE BACON FAT AS IT DRIES OUT.

A DUTCH OVEN SHOULD NEVER BE WASHED WITH SOAP. MERELY POUR IN HOT WATER TO HEAT, THEN POUR OUT. RECOAT INSIDE OF POT WITH BACON GREASE AND LEAVE FOR THE NEXT MEAL.

THE BEST PLACE TO STORE CANNED FOODS IS IN A COOL, DARK, BUT DRY SPOT.

CHECK YOUR PRESSURE COOKER MANUFACTURER'S DIRECTIONS FOR THE AMOUNT OF SPACE TO BE LEFT BETWEEN TOP OF JAR AND EACH INDIVIDUAL FOOD.

ALTHOUGH THE HOT PACK METHOD IS IN MOST COMMON USE AMONG HOME CANNERS, IT IS NOT RECOMMENDED BY THE U.S. DEPT. OF AGRICULTURE FOR LOW-ACID VEGETABLES, SUCH AS PEAS AND CARROTS, OR MEATS. PRESSURE CANNING IS THOUGHT TO BE THE ONLY SAFE WAY.

PRESSURE CANNING DOES REQUIRE A GREATER INVESTMENT, PARTICULARLY IN THE CANNER ITSELF, BUT IT'S A MUCH FASTER METHOD OF CANNING. HERE'S HOW IT'S DONE:

WARNING: WHETHER YOU USE HOT-PACK OR PRESSURE CANNING, NEVER TASTE FOOD UNTIL YOU HAVE BOILED IT FOR AT LEAST 10 MINUTES (IN SOME CASES 20 MINUTES OR MORE). IF BOILING RESULTS IN UNUSUAL ODOR OR FOAMING OR THE LIKE, DISCARD IT.

WARNING: PRESSURE CANNING UTILIZES HIGH PRESSURE and HIGH TEMPERATURES. MAKE SURE YOU READ THE OPERATING INSTRUCTIONS FOR YOUR CANNER -- AND FOLLOW THEM EXPLICITLY.

1. SELECT JARS and LIDS -- BE SURE NONE HAVE NICKS OR CRACKS. USE ONLY JARS APPROVED BY THE MANUFACTURER OF YOUR UNIT.
2. WASH AND PREPARE FOODS. (DIFFERENT FOODS MUST BE PREPARED DIFFERENTLY. INFORMATION IS AVAILABLE FROM MANUFACTURERS OF PRESSURE CANNING EQUIPMENT AS WELL AS FROM COUNTY EXTENSION or HOME ECONOMICS OFFICES.)
3. PACK FOOD INTO JARS.
4. FINISH FILLING THE JARS WITH JUICE OR SYRUP (ADD SALT IF NECESSARY).
5. WIPE THE RIM OF THE JAR FREE OF SEEDS, SALT, ETC. CLOSE LIDS.
6. SET JARS ON RACK IN PRESSURE CANNER.
7. ADD RECOMMENDED AMOUNT OF WATER.
8. CLOSE CANNER AND SET CONTROL AS RECOMMENDED.
9. PROCESS ACCORDING TO INSTRUCTIONS GIVEN FOR SPECIFIC FOOD AND FOR YOUR INDIVIDUAL CANNER.
10. WHEN CANNING IS COMPLETED, TURN OFF HEAT AND ALLOW CANNER TO COOL. USUALLY TAKES 30 MINUTES FOR THE PRESSURE TO DROP.
11. OPEN CANNER ACCORDING TO INSTRUCTIONS. KEEP OPENING SIDE AWAY FROM YOU TO ALLOW STEAM TO GO AWAY FROM YOUR FACE.
12. MAKE SURE ALL JARS ARE SEALED. DISCARD ANY THAT AREN'T SEALED ... OR RECAN.

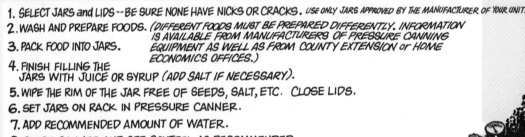

Mark Gregory

Natural Crafts

A PERFECTLY SEALED JAR IS ABSOLUTELY ESSENTIAL FOR FOOD STORAGE. TWO SEALING METHODS ARE:

1. USE A PORCELAIN-LINED ZINC CAP WITH A RUBBER RING ON A STANDARD MASON JAR.
   A. FIT RING ON JAR AND FILL JAR.
   B. SCREW CAP DOWN FIRMLY, THEN TURN BACK ¼ TURN.
   C. AFTER PROCESSING, TIGHTEN CAP.

2. USE A FLAT METAL LID AND A METAL SCREW BAND.
   A. FILL JAR, WIPE RIM CLEAN.
   B. PUT LID ON JAR.
   C. SCREW BAND ON HAND-TIGHT (THIS COMBINATION IS SELF-SEALING.)

CRACK BOOM RUMBLE

MIDWEST FOOD CELLARS WERE ALSO USED AS STORM CELLARS.

NATURAL FOODS

FOOD THAT HAS BEEN FROZEN IN A FREEZER FOR LONGER THAN THREE MONTHS CAN LOSE FLAVOR AND NUTRITION.

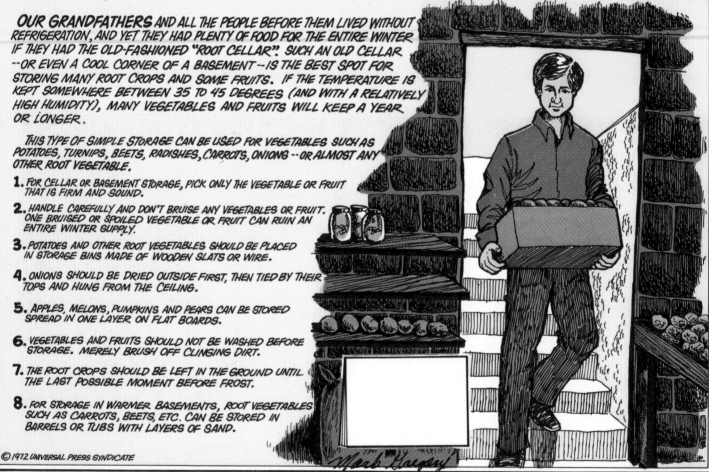

OUR GRANDFATHERS AND ALL THE PEOPLE BEFORE THEM LIVED WITHOUT REFRIGERATION, AND YET THEY HAD PLENTY OF FOOD FOR THE ENTIRE WINTER IF THEY HAD THE OLD-FASHIONED "ROOT CELLAR". SUCH AN OLD CELLAR --OR EVEN A COOL CORNER OF A BASEMENT -- IS THE BEST SPOT FOR STORING MANY ROOT CROPS AND SOME FRUITS. IF THE TEMPERATURE IS KEPT SOMEWHERE BETWEEN 35 TO 45 DEGREES (AND WITH A RELATIVELY HIGH HUMIDITY), MANY VEGETABLES AND FRUITS WILL KEEP A YEAR OR LONGER.

THIS TYPE OF SIMPLE STORAGE CAN BE USED FOR VEGETABLES SUCH AS POTATOES, TURNIPS, BEETS, RADISHES, CARROTS, ONIONS -- OR ALMOST ANY OTHER ROOT VEGETABLE.

1. FOR CELLAR OR BASEMENT STORAGE, PICK ONLY THE VEGETABLE OR FRUIT THAT IS FIRM AND SOUND.

2. HANDLE CAREFULLY AND DON'T BRUISE ANY VEGETABLES OR FRUIT. ONE BRUISED OR SPOILED VEGETABLE OR FRUIT CAN RUIN AN ENTIRE WINTER SUPPLY.

3. POTATOES AND OTHER ROOT VEGETABLES SHOULD BE PLACED IN STORAGE BINS MADE OF WOODEN SLATS OR WIRE.

4. ONIONS SHOULD BE DRIED OUTSIDE FIRST, THEN TIED BY THEIR TOPS AND HUNG FROM THE CEILING.

5. APPLES, MELONS, PUMPKINS AND PEARS CAN BE STORED SPREAD IN ONE LAYER ON FLAT BOARDS.

6. VEGETABLES AND FRUITS SHOULD NOT BE WASHED BEFORE STORAGE. MERELY BRUSH OFF CLINGING DIRT.

7. THE ROOT CROPS SHOULD BE LEFT IN THE GROUND UNTIL THE LAST POSSIBLE MOMENT BEFORE FROST.

8. FOR STORAGE IN WARMER BASEMENTS, ROOT VEGETABLES SUCH AS CARROTS, BEETS, ETC. CAN BE STORED IN BARRELS OR TUBS WITH LAYERS OF SAND.

© 1972 UNIVERSAL PRESS SYNDICATE

Mark Gregory

Natural Crafts

STORAGE IN THE GARDEN ITSELF IS THE SIMPLEST METHOD FOR VEGETABLES SUCH AS BRUSSELS SPROUTS, KALE, COLLARDS, AND PARSNIPS.

THESE CAN BE LEFT IN THE GARDEN ALL WINTER, PROVIDING FRESH VEGETABLES AS YOU NEED THEM. (THIS DOES NOT APPLY TO MANY AREAS OF THE NORTH AND CANADA.)

A PROTECTIVE MULCH SUCH AS STRAW LAID OVER WINTERING GARDEN VEGETABLES WILL HELP KEEP THEM FROM FREEZING.

SWEET CORN IS ONE OF THE FEW VEGETABLES NATIVE TO THE NORTH AMERICAN CONTINENT.

NATURAL FOODS

ANOTHER GREAT OLD-TIME RECIPE IS CORN FRITTERS.

CUT KERNELS FROM 6 EARS OF FRESH CORN RESERVING LIQUID. YOU WILL NEED 2 CUPS OF CORN and 1 CUP OF CORN LIQUID. (ADD MILK IF YOU HAVEN'T ENOUGH.)

- 1 EGG
- 1½ CUPS FLOUR
- ¾ TSP. SALT
- 2 TSP. BAKING POWDER
- 1 TSP. CINNAMON
- ⅛ TSP. NUTMEG

MIX AND FRY IN DEEP FAT (360°) ABOUT 3 MINUTES -- TURNING ONCE. DRAIN AND DIP IN CINNAMON HONEY (CINNAMON IN WARM HONEY)

DRYING SWEET CORN WAS ONE OF GRANDMA'S FAVORITE WAYS OF PRESERVING THIS DELICIOUS AND HEALTHFUL FOOD. WITH A LITTLE BIT OF TIME YOU CAN TRY THIS OLD-TIME METHOD AND PRODUCE A GREAT FOOD FOR WINTER USE THAT WILL "BRING SUMMER RIGHT BACK."

1. GATHER FRESH SWEET CORN, SELECTING ONLY EARS THAT HAVE FRESH AND GREEN HUSKS.

2. CUT THE CORN OFF THE COBS UNTIL YOU'VE COLLECTED ENOUGH FOR 8 PINTS. (DO NOT BLANCH OR COOK THE CORN.)

3. MIX IN 6 TABLESPOONS OF GRANULATED SUGAR, 4 TEASPOONS OF COARSE CANNING SALT and A HALF CUP OF SWEET CREAM.

4. BOIL FOR 20 MINUTES, STIRRING CONSTANTLY.

5. SPREAD THE COOKED CORN IN SHALLOW PANS AND PLACE IN OVEN SET AT LOWEST HEAT.

6. WHEN CORN IS DRY AND CRISPY REMOVE AND PLACE IN CLEAN BROWN PAPER SACKS. HANG THE SACKS IN A DRY ROOM AND AWAY FROM INSECTS AND PESTS. AFTER THE CORN HAS DRIED COMPLETELY IT WILL RATTLE IN THE SACKS AND CAN BE REMOVED AND STORED IN CLEAN GLASS JARS.

7. CORN PREPARED THIS WAY IS DELICIOUS ON A COLD WINTER NIGHT. JUST SIMMER IN WATER WITH BUTTER, OR MILK IF YOU PREFER, AND WATCH IT DISAPPEAR. (YOU DON'T NEED TO SOAK IT BEFORE COOKING.)

Mark Gregory

Natural Crafts

CORNCOBS CAN BE USED IN ANY NUMBER OF WAYS. GROUND UP CORNCOBS MAKE AN EXCELLENT MULCH OR MATERIAL FOR COMPOST.

CORNCOBS ALSO MAKE EXCELLENT FIRE STARTERS.

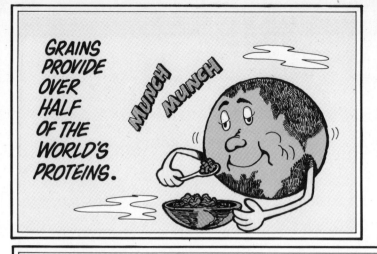

GRAINS PROVIDE OVER HALF OF THE WORLD'S PROTEINS.

MUNCH MUNCH

WHEN MAKING BREADS, MUFFINS, OR WAFFLES, ADD WHOLE CRACKED WHEAT FOR A RICH, NUTTY FLAVOR.

GRINDING YOUR OWN GRAIN IS ONE WAY OF PROVIDING YOUR FAMILY WITH LOTS OF HEALTHFUL AND NUTRITIOUS FOODS, AS WELL AS A DELICIOUS AND UNUSUAL "TREAT" SUCH AS CRACKED GRAIN BREAKFAST CEREAL, OR WHOLE-WHEAT BREADS OR MUFFINS.

YOU CAN BUY CLEANED OR UNCLEANED GRAIN FROM FARMERS, FEED & GRAIN STORES, OR HEALTH-FOOD STORES. BE SURE THAT YOU BUY GRAIN THAT IS FRESH AND NON-CHEMICALLY TREATED.

IF YOU BUY UNCLEANED GRAIN, YOU WILL HAVE TO CLEAN IT BY WINNOWING (POURING GRAINS FROM ONE CONTAINER TO ANOTHER AND ALLOWING A BREEZE OR AIR FROM A FAN TO BLOW OFF THE DIRT AND CHAFF).

WHEAT, BARLEY, SOYBEANS, MILLET, RYE, OATS, AND **RICE** ARE SOME OF THE GRAINS THAT CAN BE GROUND EASILY AT HOME USING A COFFEE MILL, HAND OR ELECTRIC MILL, OR EVEN SOME BLENDERS.

AFTER THE GRAIN HAS BEEN GROUND IT KEEPS FOR ABOUT A MONTH, THEN BEGINS TO LOSE FLAVOR.

GRAIN THAT HAS NOT YET BEEN GROUND CAN BE STORED IN CLOSED GLASS JARS KEPT IN A COOL, DRY PLACE.

GRAIN MAY BE GROUND TO ALMOST ANY FORM FROM ROUGH "CRACKED" GRAIN TO SUPERFINE FLOUR. GRINDING TO MAKE FINE FLOUR WILL USUALLY TAKE THREE OR FOUR GRINDINGS.

THE GRAINS MAY BE USED IN ALL SORTS OF WAYS, BOTH WHOLE OR GROUND, FOR CEREALS OR BAKING ALL KINDS OF GOODIES.

FOR A REALLY UNUSUAL CEREAL TRY MIXING SEVERAL KINDS OF CRACKED GRAINS TOGETHER.

WHEAT

Mark Gregory

Natural Crafts

TO CLEAN GRAIN, POUR IT ON A "WINNOWING SCREEN." SHAKE IT TO REMOVE THE DUST AND CHAFF. REMOVE ANY HEAVY GRIT BY HAND. DO THIS ON A WINDY DAY, AND MOST OF THE CHAFF WILL FLY AWAY.

YOU CAN EASILY MAKE A WINNOWING FRAME FROM 1 x 2's AND NEW WINDOW SCREEN WIRE PURCHASED AT ANY HARDWARE STORE.

A SOURDOUGH STARTER KEPT IN THE FAMILY AND HANDED DOWN FROM GENERATION TO GENERATION IS A HERITAGE ANYONE WOULD BE HAPPY TO RECEIVE.

NATURAL FOODS

A REAL TREAT FOR PIONEER CHILDREN WAS SNOW ICE CREAM. TRY IT, YOU'LL BE PLEASANTLY SURPRISED. GATHER ONLY FRESH, CLEAN SNOW. TO A FULL BOWL STIR IN SUGAR, CANNED MILK OR WHOLE CREAM AND YOUR FAVORITE FLAVORING TO TASTE. Eat immediately.

Mention the word "sourdough" AND RUGGED GOLD MINERS CARRYING THEIR MEAGER SUPPLIES AND PROSPECTING ALASKA AND THE YUKON FOR GOLD IMMEDIATELY COME TO MIND. AS ROMANTIC AS THE NAME IS, SOURDOUGH IS AS PRACTICAL, EASY-TO-MAKE AND TASTY TODAY AS IT WAS BACK IN 1849.

There are literally thousands of recipes FOR MAKING YOUR OWN "SOUR-DOUGH CULTURE" OR STARTER. HERE ARE TWO WAYS YOU CAN MAKE YOURS. THE FIRST IS MADE WITHOUT YEAST JUST AS THE OLD-TIME PROS-PECTORS DID. THE SECOND IS A MORE MODERN VERSION MADE WITH YEAST AND IS FASTER TO MAKE.

IN USING YOUR SOURDOUGH STARTER, ALWAYS LEAVE ABOUT A CUP TO CONTINUE THE STRAIN. TO THIS ADD ENOUGH FLOUR AND WATER TO BRING BACK TO THE ORIGINAL LEVEL -- THEN REFRIGERATE.

Recipe #1

IN AN EARTHENWARE CROCK PLACE FOUR CUPS OF FLOUR, TWO TABLE-SPOONS OF SUGAR AND A TABLE-SPOON OF VINEGAR. ADD ENOUGH WATER TO MAKE A LIGHT CREAMY BATTER. COVER THIS LOOSELY WITH A CHEESECLOTH AND LEAVE IN A WARM SPOT. THE MIXTURE SHOULD BE READY FOR USE IN 7 TO 10 DAYS. IF PROPERLY WORKING, THE STARTER WILL BUBBLE AND "WORK" GIVING OFF A PLEASANT, SLIGHTLY SOUR SMELL.

Recipe #2

IF YOU WANT TO CHEAT A LITTLE, A MODERN VERSION IS FASTER. SIMPLY DISSOLVE ONE PACKAGE OF DRY YEAST IN TWO CUPS OF WARM WATER. MIX IN ABOUT TWO CUPS OF FLOUR AND LEAVE OVERNIGHT IN A WARM SPOT.

SOURDOUGH BREAD

PLACE ALL OF YOUR STARTER MIX, EXCEPT FOR ABOUT A CUP (which will be used to replenish your starter) IN A LARGE MIXING BOWL. ADD ONE TABLESPOON OF COOKING OIL AND A PINCH OF BAKING SODA. ADD ENOUGH FLOUR TO MAKE A BOUNCY, SLICK DOUGH. THE SECRET WITH SOURDOUGH BREAD IS TO KNEAD VERY LITTLE. SHAPE INTO LOAVES AND PLACE IN A WARM SPOT UNTIL IT RISES. BAKE IN A 375° OVEN ABOUT 45 MINUTES UNTIL CRUST BROWNS AND LOAVES' SOUND HOLLOW WHEN TAPPED.

Biscuits

FOR BISCUITS, USE THE SAME INGRED-IENTS AS IN BREAD, BUT ADD ENOUGH FLOUR TO MAKE A STIFF DOUGH. DON'T LET THE DOUGH RISE, BUT QUICKLY ROLL IT OUT AND POP INTO A HOT (425°) OVEN FOR 10 TO 12 MINUTES.

Natural Crafts

A Bottle Garden will bring a touch of the outdoors to your indoors.

1. FOR THE BOTTLE YOU CAN USE A BRANDY GOBLET, FISH BOWL, OR EVEN AN OLD "FRUIT" OR CANNING JAR.

2. PLACE A LAYER OF SAND, A LAYER OF SOIL AND, PERHAPS, AN UNUSUAL ROCK IN THE BOTTLE. MOISTEN THE SOIL, BEING CAREFUL NOT TO SPLASH UP ON THE GLASS SIDES OF THE JAR OR BOTTLE.

3. THEN COMES THE FUN. PLANT MINIATURE VINES, FERNS, EVEN GRASS SEEDS OR EVERGREEN SEEDLINGS IN YOUR "GARDEN." BITS OF MOSS ADD INTEREST AROUND THE PLANTS.

4. KEEP THIS "INDOOR WOODS" OUT OF DIRECT SUN. BE SURE TO KEEP THE SOIL MOIST. A GLASS COVER OVER THE BOWL WILL CONSERVE MOISTURE.

BECOME **SELF-SUFFICIENT** -- LEARN TO LIVE FROM THE PRODUCTS OF **YOUR OWN LABORS.**

NATURAL FOODS

YOGURT IS ONE OF THE HIGHEST PROTEIN FOODS, AND IS EASY TO DIGEST. YOGURT MADE FROM GOATS' MILK IS EVEN BETTER, EASIER TO DIGEST, THAN THAT MADE FROM COWS' MILK. YOGURT IS ALSO EXTREMELY LOW IN CALORIES.

TODAY'S SEARCH FOR HEALTHFUL, NATURAL FOODS HAS PUT A NEW FOCUS ON YOGURT, ONE OF THE OLDEST NATURAL FOODS. IF YOU HAVEN'T TRIED YOGURT YET, NOW'S THE TIME. THIS HEALTHFUL AND DELIGHTFUL FOOD IS NOT ONLY EASY TO MAKE AT HOME -- IT'S VERY ECONOMICAL.

TO GROW YOUR OWN YOGURT, YOU WILL NEED A STARTER MIX AVAILABLE FROM NATURAL FOOD STORES. YOGURT IS JUST LIKE SOURDOUGH BREAD IN THAT YOU MUST KEEP A BIT OF IT TO USE AS A STARTER TO PERPETUATE YOUR CULTURE AND KEEP IT GOING.

IT'S easy to make YOUR own Yogurt
IF YOU FOLLOW THESE SIMPLE STEPS:

1. HEAT ONE QUART OF FRESH MILK (THE MILK SHOULD BE WARMED -- *BUT NOT ALLOWED TO BOIL*)

2. ALLOW THE MILK TO COOL TO LUKEWARM TEMPERATURE.

3. PLACE ONE TABLESPOON OF YOGURT STARTER-MIX IN THE BOTTOM OF A COUPLE OF MEDIUM-SIZE (pint) JARS. THE JARS MUST FIRST BE STERILIZED IN BOILING WATER, THEN ALLOWED TO DRY THOROUGHLY. THEY SHOULD HAVE TIGHT-SEALING LIDS.

© 1972 Universal Press Syndicate

4. SLOWLY POUR THE HEATED MILK INTO THE JARS.

5. PLACE THE LIDS ON THE JARS AND CLOSE TIGHTLY. PLACE THE JARS IN A WARM SPOT WITH CONSTANT TEMPERATURE, SUCH AS IN FRONT OF A HEAT REGISTER. OR YOU CAN PLACE THE JARS IN A LARGE KETTLE, POUR IN WARM WATER AND KEEP CHANGING IT TO KEEP A FAIRLY CONSTANT TEMPERATURE. YOGURT IS READY WHEN THE LIQUID HAS CONGEALED -- ABOUT 4 to 6 HOURS.

THE YOGURT IS THEN KEPT REFRIGERATED FOR USE. IT WILL THICKEN AND CONGEAL A BIT WHEN COOL.

If you really get "into" YOGURT...
YOU'LL WANT TO BUY A CULTURIZING UNIT. THIS LITTLE DEVICE HAS AN ELECTRICALLY HEATED BASE ON WHICH SITS PYREX GLASS CONTAINERS, AND MAKES KEEPING THE CULTURE A CONSTANT TEMPERATURE A SNAP.

Mark Gregory

YOGURT IS DELIGHTFUL SERVED CHILLED BY ITSELF, OR YOU CAN COMBINE IT WITH ALMOST ANY KIND OF TANGY FRUIT OR BERRY SUCH AS ORANGES, LEMON, BLUEBERRIES, PINEAPPLES, GRAPES, ETC. FRUIT AND BERRIES SHOULD BE FRESH. JUST MASH OR PUREE AND MIX WITH YOGURT.

YOGURT ALSO MAKES AN EXCELLENT **SALAD DRESSING** FOR FRESH GARDEN-VEGETABLE SALADS. MERELY ADD ROQUEFORT OR BLEU CHEESE, AND WHATEVER OTHER INGREDIENTS YOU LIKE. TRY A BIT OF DRY MUSTARD, GRATED HORSERADISH OR CHOPPED CHIVES.

PRODUCING GOOD MAPLE SYRUP FROM SAP REQUIRES PATIENCE.

MAPLE SYRUP CAN BE USED AS A GREAT NATURAL PANCAKE SYRUP, OR IN HUNDREDS OF CANDY RECIPES.

IN OLDEN TIMES ONE OF THE RITUALS OF EARLY SPRING WAS "SUGARING TIME" OR GATHERING SAP FROM SUGAR MAPLES TO PRODUCE MAPLE SUGAR OR SYRUP.

ALTHOUGH IT IS PRIMARILY PRACTICED NOW ONLY IN THE NORTHEASTERN PORTION OF NORTH AMERICA, IT WAS ONCE PRACTICED WIDELY BY THE PIONEERS AND INDIANS TO GATHER THE MUCH NEEDED SWEETENING. ALTHOUGH SUGAR MAPLES PRODUCE THE MOST AND BEST SAP, ALMOST ALL OTHER MAPLES WILL ALSO PRODUCE SUGAR SAP, AS WELL AS OTHER TYPES OF TREES INCLUDING BLACK BIRCH.

EXTRACTING SUGAR OR SYRUP FROM SAP IS A LOT OF WORK, BUT PRODUCES A NATURAL SWEETENER THAT IS HARD TO BEAT.

IT TAKES ABOUT 30 TO 40 GALLONS OF RAW SAP TO PRODUCE ONE GALLON OF SYRUP, AND ONE "TAP" FROM A MEDIUM SIZE TREE (ONE AT LEAST 12 INCHES IN DIAMETER) WILL PRODUCE ABOUT 20 GALLONS OF SAP.

SAP GATHERING TIME CAN BE ANYTIME FROM THE MIDDLE OF FEBRUARY TO APRIL DEPENDING ON THE CLIMATE AND LOCATION. IT USUALLY STARTS WITH THE FIRST GOOD THAW, AND THE BEST SAP PRODUCING DAYS ARE WARM AND SUNNY FOLLOWING A FROSTY NIGHT. MAKE AN EXPERIMENTAL HOLE AND WATCH FOR THE FIRST SIGN OF SAP OOZING.

SAP GATHERING IS SIMPLE:

1. A HOLE IS DRILLED INTO THE TREE ABOUT THREE FEET OFF THE GROUND AND ON THE SUNNY SIDE. THE HOLE IS TILTED UPWARD AND IS FROM TWO TO THREE INCHES IN DEPTH. A SPIGOT IS GENTLY HAMMERED IN PLACE AND A BUCKET PLACED ON THE SPIGOT. FROM THEN ON IT IS A MATTER OF EMPTYING BUCKETS.

2. TO MAKE SYRUP FROM THE SAP, BOIL IT DOWN. THIS TAKES PLENTY OF TIME AND A LOT OF WATCHING TO MAKE SURE THE SAP DOESN'T BOIL OVER AND SCORCH.

WHEN THE SYRUP REACHES THE RIGHT CONSISTENCY AND TASTE TO SUIT YOU, REMOVE IT FROM THE FIRE AND POUR INTO CLEAN CONTAINERS.

ALTHOUGH YOU CAN BOIL DOWN THE SAP ON YOUR KITCHEN STOVE, IT'S EASIER ON AN OUTSIDE FIRE AND USING A LARGE KETTLE OR HOME-MADE METAL "BOILER". (YOU CAN USE A CANDY THERMOMETER TO HELP IN DETERMINING THE CONSISTENCY. WHEN SAP FIRST BOILS, NOTE THE TEMPERATURE. WHEN THE TEMPERATURE RISES 7°, IT HAS THE RIGHT SUGAR CONSISTENCY.)

© 1973 UNIVERSAL PRESS SYNDICATE

YOU CAN EASILY MAKE YOUR OWN SPIGOTS FROM ELDERBERRY STEMS.

CUT LARGE STEMS INTO 5 INCH LENGTHS AND REMOVE THE SOFT PITH USING A COAT HANGER WIRE. SHARPEN ONE END TO DRIVE INTO THE HOLE IN THE TREE AND CUT A NOTCH FOR HANGING THE SAP BUCKET.

OLD-TIME SMOKED FISH WAS TOUGH and SALTY, BUT WAS USED AS A STAPLE FOOD ON SAILING VESSELS and BY MOST EXPLORERS.

NATURAL FOODS

YOU CAN EASILY MAKE A SMOKED FISH SANDWICH BY MIXING MAYONNAISE WITH FINELY CHOPPED SMOKED FISH AND SEASONING TO SUIT YOUR OWN TASTES.

SMOKING IS AN EXCELLENT AND FUN WAY OF PREPARING AND PRESERVING MOST ANY SALT OR FRESH-WATER FISH. ALL IT TAKES IS AN EASILY-MADE HOME SMOKER AND A LOT OF PATIENCE. THE RESULTS ARE WELL WORTH IT.

YOU CAN EASILY MAKE YOUR OWN SMOKING OVEN FROM A METAL BARREL AS SHOWN. (MAKE SURE IT HASN'T BEEN USED TO STORE POISONOUS CHEMICALS, NOR THAT IT'S COATED ON THE INSIDE WITH SUCH CHEMICALS.)

USE ONLY FRESHLY CAUGHT FISH AND CLEAN THEM AS SOON AS POSSIBLE. SMALL FISH CAN BE SMOKED WHOLE, JUST SCALE, REMOVE THE INTERNAL ORGANS, and WASH OFF THE SLIME WITH A MIXTURE OF HALF VINEGAR AND HALF WATER. ON LARGER FISH REMOVE THE HEAD, GILLS, FINS and INTERNAL ORGANS. SPLIT IN HALF, REMOVE THE BACKBONE. LEAVE ON THE TAIL AND SKIN. WASH THOROUGHLY TO REMOVE ALL BLOOD.

FRESH CUT GREEN HARDWOOD IS GOOD AS IT WILL SMOLDER and SMOKE PROPERLY. HARDWOOD SAWDUST ADDED TO A CHARCOAL OR BRIQUET FIRE WILL WORK AS WELL. KEEP THE TEMPERATURE IN THE OVEN BETWEEN 70° and 85°. FISH SMOKED PROPERLY FOR 24 HOURS SHOULD KEEP FOR 2 WEEKS; SMOKED FOR 2 DAYS IT SHOULD KEEP 4 WEEKS. SMOKED FISH SHOULD BE KEPT DRY AND COLD. REFRIGERATE, BUT DO NOT FREEZE.

CAUTION: TO INSURE A SAFE, EDIBLE FOOD, THE DIRECTIONS SHOULD BE FOLLOWED VERY CAREFULLY AND ANY OLD OR OTHERWISE SUSPECT MEAT SHOULD BE DISCARDED.

1. FIRST STEP IS TO SOAK FISH IN A BRINE SOLUTION MADE UP OF:
- 4 GALLONS OF WATER
- 8 CUPS OF SALT (5 LBS.)
- ½ LB. HONEY
- 1½ CUPS LEMON JUICE
- CRUSHED GARLIC and ONION
- 2 TABLESPOONS OF DILL

SOAK THE FISH IN THIS SOLUTION FOR 30 MINUTES FOR FISH UNDER ¼ POUND. ON LARGER FISH ADD 15 MINUTES BRINE TIME FOR EACH ¼ POUND OF FISH. IF FISH ARE NOT SKINNED ADD 25% BRINE TIME.

2. REMOVE FROM BRINE, RINSE IN FRESH WATER AND HANG TO DRY IN A COOL, DRY, BREEZY SPOT FOR 3 HOURS OR MORE.

3. PLACE IN SMOKE OVEN. SMALL FISH MAY BE HUNG BY INSERTING STICKS THROUGH GILLS AND MOUTH. LARGE FILLETS OF FISH SHOULD BE LAID ON A GRILL WITH SKIN SIDE DOWN.

START A GOOD, BUT SMALL CHARCOAL BRIQUET FIRE AS SHOWN, THEN ADD THIN SLICES OR TINY PIECES OF HARDWOOD (WOOD FROM A TREE THAT SHEDS ITS LEAVES IN WINTER) -- HICKORY, OAK, APPLE, ETC.

© 1972 UNIVERSAL PRESS SYNDICATE

LID PROPPED UP FOR DRAFT

THERMOMETER

BARBECUE GRILL GRATE

PIPE

CONT'D. ABOVE ↗

Mark Gregory

Natural Crafts

FISH MAY BE FROZEN and STORED FOR LONG TIMES, BUT IT MAY "FREEZER BURN" QUITE EASILY UNLESS PROPERLY STORED. FOR SMALL FISH PLACE IN A MILK CARTON OF WATER AND FREEZE SOLID.

MILK

LARGER FISH MAY BE QUICK FROZEN LYING ON WAXED PAPER, THEN DIPPED IN A PAN OF COLD WATER and REFROZEN. DIPPING AND FREEZING SEVERAL TIMES WILL FORM A LAYER OF ICE TO PROTECT THE FLESH. WRAP IN WAXED PAPER or PLASTIC BAGS.

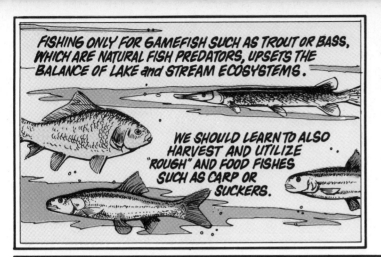

FISHING ONLY FOR GAMEFISH SUCH AS TROUT OR BASS, WHICH ARE NATURAL FISH PREDATORS, UPSETS THE BALANCE OF LAKE and STREAM ECOSYSTEMS.

WE SHOULD LEARN TO ALSO HARVEST AND UTILIZE "ROUGH" AND FOOD FISHES SUCH AS CARP OR SUCKERS.

NATURAL FOODS

FOR A REAL GOURMET "APPETIZER," TRY PICKLED FISH CHUNKS SERVED COLD IN A COCKTAIL SAUCE TO WHICH IS ADDED LEMON JUICE AND LOTS OF HORSERADISH.

MANY FISH

ARE CONSIDERED INEDIBLE BECAUSE THEY'RE MUDDY TASTING, OILY, COARSE AND FULL OF TINY BONES. PICKLING IS AN EXCELLENT WAY OF PREPARING THESE ROUGH FISH SUCH AS SUCKERS, CARP, PERCH, HERRING, SMELT and MACKEREL. USING AN OLD-TIME PICKLING RECIPE YOU CAN REMOVE THE MUDDY TASTE, SOFTEN THE BONES, AND TURN THE "WASTE" FISH INTO NATURAL GOURMET DELIGHTS.

FISH FOR PICKLING MUST BE FRESH. THEY SHOULD BE SKINNED AND GUTTED, THE HEADS and TAILS REMOVED. THE DRESSED FISH SHOULD BE WASHED THOROUGHLY IN CLEAN WATER and CUT UP INTO BITE-SIZE PIECES. IT TAKES ABOUT 4 to 5 POUNDS OF FISH CHUNKS TO MAKE UP ONE GALLON OF PICKLED FISH.

1 SOAK THE FISH PIECES IN A BRINE SOLUTION MADE OF ONE-HALF CUP PURE GRANULATED NON-IODIZED SALT PER QUART of WATER. MAKE SURE ALL PIECES ARE COVERED, AND USE A PLASTIC BUCKET FOR THE SOLUTION. ALLOW TO SOAK FOR TWO DAYS.

2 DRAIN THE PIECES ON PAPER TOWELS and RINSE THOROUGHLY TO REMOVE ALL THE BRINE.

3 MAKE UP A MIXTURE OF 1½ QUARTS WATER and 1½ QUARTS CLEAR DISTILLED VINEGAR. ADD A HALF CUP OF BROWN SUGAR and A PACKAGE OF PICKLING SPICES OR A PICKLING SPICE MIX SUCH AS THIS ONE:
PUT IN A HALF TEASPOON EACH, ALLSPICE, CLOVES, MUSTARD SEED, PEPPERCORNS, TARRAGON. ADD A STALK OF CELERY, FRESH PARSLEY, BAY LEAVES and LEMON PEEL.
BRING THE MIXTURE TO A SIMMER and SIMMER 15 MINUTES.

4 ADD FISH PIECES and SIMMER FOR 15 MINUTES or UNTIL A FORK WILL PIERCE THE FISH.

5 DRAIN OFF LIQUID and ALLOW TO COOL.

6 PACK FISH PIECES IN A CLEAN GALLON JAR (SUCH AS A GALLON MAYONNAISE JAR). PACK FISH WITH ALTERNATING LAYERS OF WHITE ONION SLICES. LEAVE SPACE AT TOP OF LAYERS.

7 POUR IN COOLED LIQUID, SHAKE TO BRING BUBBLES TO TOP, ALLOW TO SET FOR A COUPLE OF WEEKS, THEN TASTE.

KEEP REFRIGERATED. DON'T KEEP LONGER THAN 3 MONTHS!

Mark Gregory

Natural Crafts

BOW FISHING IS AN EXCELLENT and FUN WAY OF HARVESTING ROUGH FISH SUCH AS CARP, BUFFALO and "ALLIGATOR" GAR.

THE BOWFISHERMAN COMBINES BOTH THE SPORT OF ARCHERY and FISHING, AND CAN BE A HELP IN CONTROLLING THE OVERCROWDING OF ROUGH FISH IN THE NEW, BIG, MAN-MADE LAKES.

APPLES   10¢

WE HAVE BECOME TOO "BLEMISH CONSCIOUS" ABOUT FRUITS and VEGETABLES.

NATURAL FOODS

AN EXCELLENT NATURAL SALAD DRESSING CAN BE MADE WITH HOME-MADE VINEGAR. MERELY ADD TOGETHER EQUAL PARTS OF HONEY, OIL AND VINEGAR.

ONE OLD-FASHIONED KITCHEN CRAFT IS FUN AND EASY AND WILL MAKE YOU A REAL HIT WITH YOUR GOURMET FRIENDS. MAKE YOUR OWN VINEGAR.

VINEGAR CAN BE MADE FROM ALMOST ANY TART, JUICY FRUIT SUCH AS APPLES, PEARS, OR EVEN GRAPES, BUT THE MOST POPULAR IS MADE FROM APPLES. THE GREAT THING IS THAT THE APPLES OR FRUITS DON'T HAVE TO BE PERFECT, AND A BATCH OF VINEGAR IS A GOOD WAY TO UTILIZE FRUITS THAT WERE TOO BLEMISHED TO CAN OR EAT FRESH.

1. CUT APPLES INTO SMALL CHUNKS: SKINS, CORES, STEMS and ALL.

2. MASH THESE INTO A MUSH. AN EASY WAY IS IN A CLEAN, LARGE EARTHENWARE CROCK AND USING THE END OF A 2 x 4.

3. WHEN THE FRUIT IS THOROUGHLY MASHED, COVER THE CROCK WITH A PIECE OF AN OLD SHEET OR TOWEL, TYING IT ON TIGHTLY TO KEEP THE GNATS OUT.

4. PLACE THE CROCK IN A BASEMENT OR OTHER ROOM WITH A CONSTANT and MODERATE TEMPERATURE. ALLOW THE BREW TO AGE FOR 5 OR 6 MONTHS.

5. OCCASIONALLY STIR AND TASTE THE VINEGAR. WHEN IT SUITS YOUR TASTE, STRAIN THE LIQUID OFF INTO CLEAN GLASS JARS.

6. STORE YOUR HOME-MADE VINEGAR IN A COOL DARK PLACE. (CAUTION: DON'T TIGHTEN THE LIDS TOO TIGHTLY ON THE JUGS.)

Mark Gregory

Natural Crafts

HOME-MADE VINEGAR CAN EASILY BE MADE INTO A REAL "GOURMET VINEGAR," BY MERELY ADDING HERBS TO THE LIQUID.
EXPERIMENT WITH YOUR FAVORITE HERBS TO MAKE A VINEGAR TO SUIT YOUR TASTE.

MINT VINEG

1. PLACE A CUP OF DRIED HERBS IN A PINT OF VINEGAR. PLACE THE LID ON THE JAR AND PLACE IN A WARM DRY SPOT SUCH AS A SUNNY WINDOW.

2. ALLOW TO SET FOR A COUPLE OF WEEKS. STIRRING OR SHAKING DAILY WILL HELP.

3. WHEN THE VINEGAR SUITS YOUR TASTE, POUR IT OFF INTO JUGS AND STORE IN A COOL DARK SPOT.

4

HUNTING

AND FISHING

THERE ARE MORE WHITE-TAILED DEER TODAY IN NORTH AMERICA THAN WHEN THE WHITE MAN FIRST ARRIVED HERE.

THROUGH THEIR LOVE OF THE OUTDOORS, THE SPORTSMEN OF THE WORLD WERE THE FIRST TO NOTICE AND EXPRESS CONCERN FOR THE ILL EFFECTS OF AN EXPANDING CIVILIZATION ON FOREST, FIELD and STREAM.

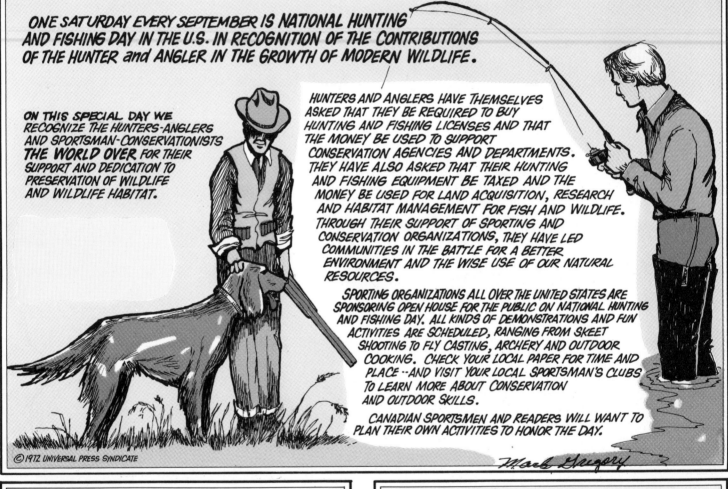

ONE SATURDAY EVERY SEPTEMBER IS NATIONAL HUNTING AND FISHING DAY IN THE U.S. IN RECOGNITION OF THE CONTRIBUTIONS OF THE HUNTER and ANGLER IN THE GROWTH OF MODERN WILDLIFE.

ON THIS SPECIAL DAY WE RECOGNIZE THE HUNTERS-ANGLERS AND SPORTSMAN-CONSERVATIONISTS THE WORLD OVER FOR THEIR SUPPORT AND DEDICATION TO PRESERVATION OF WILDLIFE AND WILDLIFE HABITAT.

HUNTERS AND ANGLERS HAVE THEMSELVES ASKED THAT THEY BE REQUIRED TO BUY HUNTING AND FISHING LICENSES AND THAT THE MONEY BE USED TO SUPPORT CONSERVATION AGENCIES AND DEPARTMENTS. THEY HAVE ALSO ASKED THAT THEIR HUNTING AND FISHING EQUIPMENT BE TAXED AND THE MONEY BE USED FOR LAND ACQUISITION, RESEARCH AND HABITAT MANAGEMENT FOR FISH AND WILDLIFE. THROUGH THEIR SUPPORT OF SPORTING AND CONSERVATION ORGANIZATIONS, THEY HAVE LED COMMUNITIES IN THE BATTLE FOR A BETTER ENVIRONMENT AND THE WISE USE OF OUR NATURAL RESOURCES.

SPORTING ORGANIZATIONS ALL OVER THE UNITED STATES ARE SPONSORING OPEN HOUSE FOR THE PUBLIC ON NATIONAL HUNTING AND FISHING DAY. ALL KINDS OF DEMONSTRATIONS AND FUN ACTIVITIES ARE SCHEDULED, RANGING FROM SKEET SHOOTING TO FLY CASTING, ARCHERY AND OUTDOOR COOKING. CHECK YOUR LOCAL PAPER FOR TIME AND PLACE -- AND VISIT YOUR LOCAL SPORTSMAN'S CLUBS TO LEARN MORE ABOUT CONSERVATION AND OUTDOOR SKILLS.

CANADIAN SPORTSMEN AND READERS WILL WANT TO PLAN THEIR OWN ACTIVITIES TO HONOR THE DAY.

Mack Gregory

HUNTERS AND FISHERMEN SPEND COUNTLESS MILLIONS EACH YEAR ON THE LICENSES, PERMITS and TAXES ON SPORTING ARMS AND AMMUNITION.

IN THE U.S. THIS MONEY IS USED FOR LAND ACQUISITION, RESEARCH and WILDLIFE MANAGEMENT ONLY. IT BENEFITS THE NON-HUNTING PUBLIC AS WELL AS THE HUNTER AND NON-GAME ANIMALS AS WELL AS GAME ANIMALS.

IN ONE WAY OR ANOTHER MONEY FROM HUNTING AND FISHING LICENSES PROVIDES FOR WILDLIFE MANAGEMENT AND PRESERVATION. ALMOST 3 MILLION HUNTING LICENSES ARE SOLD EACH YEAR IN CANADA ALONE.

LIKE MANY WILDLIFE LOW ON THE FOOD CHAIN, RABBITS HAVE AN EXTREMELY HIGH POPULATION TURN-OVER EACH WINTER (SOMETIMES AS HIGH AS 80 PER CENT)

THIS TURN-OVER DEPENDS ON TWO THINGS -- CARRYING CAPACITY OF THEIR HABITAT, AND THE WINTER WEATHER CONDITIONS.

NATURAL FOODS

HASENPFEFFER

MARINATE ONE CLEANED AND CUT-UP RABBIT FOR 24 HOURS IN THE FOLLOWING MIXTURE:

- EQUAL PARTS VINEGAR and WATER
- 2 TSP. PICKLING SPICES
- 1 ONION SLICED
- 3 TSP. SUGAR
- SALT and PEPPER

SIMMER RABBIT IN MARINADE UNTIL TENDER (ABOUT 1½ HOURS).
REMOVE RABBIT and THICKEN JUICE FOR GRAVY.

IN DAYS PAST MANY A YOUNGSTER SPENT THE HOURS BEFORE "SUNRISE" AND AFTER SCHOOL TENDING HIS "RABBIT TRAPS." ALTHOUGH THIS WAS PRIMARILY MEANT TO BE A MEANS OF INCOME FOR THE YOUNGSTER, IT WAS REALLY A "LIFE-LESSON" IN NATURE ON HOW "WILD" CREATURES LIVED.

UNFORTUNATELY, THERE ARE FEW YOUNGSTERS TODAY WHO HAVE HAD THE OPPORTUNITY TO ENJOY THIS EXPERIENCE. FORTUNATELY, THERE ARE PLENTY OF RABBITS, AND IT'S STILL A GREAT WAY OF TEACHING A YOUNGSTER SOME "NATURAL WOODSMANSHIP," AS WELL AS A LITTLE "NATURAL SCIENCE."

TRAPPING RABBITS IS ALSO A GREAT WAY OF KEEPING THEM AWAY FROM VALUABLE TREES AND SHRUBS, AS WELL AS PROVIDING AN OCCASIONAL OLD-TIME DISH OF "HASENPFEFFER." (MAKE SURE YOU CHECK WITH LOCAL GAME LAWS REGARDING TRAPPING AND SEASONS.)

THE TRADITIONAL MANNER OF TRAPPING RABBITS UTILIZES A SIMPLE BOX TRAP. THIS CAN EASILY BE BUILT FROM SCRAP LUMBER.

BOX TRAPS ARE MOST EFFICIENT WHEN PLACED ON A REGULAR RABBIT PATH. FARM BOYS PLACED THEM ALONG OVERGROWN FENCE ROWS -- A FAVORITE SPOT OF RABBITS. OR PLACE THEM AT THE EDGE OF YOUR GARDEN OR NEAR A YOUNG FRUIT ORCHARD.

THE TRAPS MUST BE CHECKED AT LEAST TWICE A DAY. DO NOT LEAVE SET TRAPS UNATTENDED FOR ANY LENGTH OF TIME. ALWAYS SPRING THE TRAPS IF YOU WON'T BE TRAPPING FOR SOME TIME.

ANOTHER LESSON MANY A SCHOOL BOY HAS LEARNED THE HARD WAY IS NOT TO RUN YOUR BARE HAND INTO A SPRUNG TRAP WITHOUT LOOKING. A VERY ANGRY TOMCAT OR SKUNK CAN CAUSE A LOT OF TROUBLE.

© 1972 UNIVERSAL PRESS SYNDICATE

Mark Gregory

Natural Crafts

ADEQUATE FOOD AND COVER ARE THE MOST IMPORTANT FACTORS IN A RABBIT POPULATION. IF YOU WANT MORE RABBITS IN YOUR AREA, TRY BEING A LESS NEAT "LANDSKEEPER" OR GARDENER.

ALLOW WEEDS TO GROW AROUND THE PERIMETER OF YOUR PROPERTY. PLACE A BRUSHPILE WITHIN EASY HOPPING DISTANCE OF AN OVERGROWN FENCE OR OTHER NATURAL RABBIT PATH.

EVEN THE TINIEST STREAM IS A THRIVING COMMUNITY OF LIFE, EACH SPECIES DEPENDING ON THE OTHER FOR SURVIVAL, SO IF YOU REMOVE BAIT, FROGS, FISH OR WHATEVER, TAKE ONLY WHAT YOU NEED.

MINNOW SCHOOL

1 + 3 = 4

NATURAL FOODS

"HUSH PUPPIES" FRIED IN THE SKILLET AFTER FRYING FISH IS A MOUTH-WATERING DELIGHT. MIX TOGETHER 2 CUPS CORNMEAL, 1 CUP WATER, 1 TSP SALT, DROP BY SPOON INTO THE HOT FAT AND FRY TILL CRISP.

A **FISHING HOLE** and **LAZY SUMMER DAYS** JUST SEEM TO GO TOGETHER LIKE A BAREFOOT BOY AND A FISHING POLE. SO FIND A GOOD FISHING HOLE, A CAN OF NATURAL BAITS AND **RELAX**.

COLLECTING NATURAL BAITS FOR FISHING CAN BE AS MUCH FUN AS THE FISHING.

EARTHWORMS ARE THE NUMBER ONE NATURAL BAIT FOR MANY KINDS OF FISH. LOOK FOR THEM UNDER THE EDGES OF MANURE PILES...OR IN DAMP SPOTS ALONG CREEK BANKS.

YOU CAN FIND NIGHT CRAWLERS (A LARGE EARTHWORM) AT NIGHTTIME BY SHINING A BRIGHT LIGHT THROUGH FRESHLY-CUT GRASS -- OR ALMOST ANYTIME JUST AFTER A RAIN SHOWER.

INSECTS FOUND ALONG A STREAM OR LAKE BANK ARE EXCELLENT BAIT. GRASSHOPPERS OR CRICKETS ARE GOOD EXAMPLES. THEY ARE EASILY CAUGHT VERY EARLY IN THE MORNING WHILE THEY'RE STILL SOMEWHAT SLUGGISH FROM THE COOLNESS.

ALL THE TINY UNDERWATER CREATURES SUCH AS CADDIS WORMS, OR HELGRAMMITES ARE ALSO EXCELLENT BAIT FOR USE IN STREAM FISHING.

TO COLLECT THEM, HOLD A PIECE OF SCREEN WIRE DOWNSTREAM AND TURN OVER ROCKS UPSTREAM. THE "BAIT" WILL BE SWEPT INTO THE SCREEN WIRE BY THE CURRENT.

AND, OF COURSE, MINNOWS and SMALL CRAWFISH ARE AMONG THE BEST OF NATURAL BAITS. THEY MAY BE NETTED OR TRAPPED (SEE LOCAL GAME LAWS REGARDING LEGAL METHODS OF OBTAINING WILD MINNOWS.)

Natural Crafts

ONE OF THE EASIEST WAYS TO CATCH MINNOWS IS IN A HOMEMADE MINNOW TRAP BAITED WITH BREAD CRUMBS AND PLACED IN A DEEP POOL OF A SHALLOW, CLEAR STREAM.

THE MINNOW TRAP MAY BE MADE USING A GALLON FRUIT JAR AND A FUNNEL MADE OF SCREEN WIRE PLACED OVER THE OPENINGS IN THE FRUIT JAR.

REMOVING SUCH PROLIFIC FISH AS THE PERCH AND OTHER SUNFISHES HELPS KEEP A LAKE OR POND IN BALANCE.

ONE OF THE EASIEST FISH TO CATCH DURING THE WINTER IS PERCH, AND COOKED PROPERLY, THEY'RE EXCELLENT. SKIN AND REMOVE THE FINS, HEAD AND INSIDES. SHAKE THE CLEANED PERCH IN A BAG OF FLOUR, THEN DROP IN SMOKING HOT COOKING OIL. BROWN BOTH SIDES QUICKLY. SERVE PIPING HOT WITH LOTS OF TARTAR SAUCE.

IF YOU WANT TO BEAT THE WINTER DOLDRUMS AND PROVIDE A WINTER FEAST AS WELL, TRY ICE FISHING.

THE FIRST STEP IS TO FIND A GOOD LAKE OR POND WITH PLENTY OF PERCH, CRAPPIE OR PANFISH.

MAKE SURE YOU CHECK THE ICE ON THE LAKE. IT SHOULD BE AT LEAST 5 OR 6 INCHES THICK AND CLEAR TO SUPPORT AN ADULT.

YOU'LL NEED AN AXE OR A SPECIAL HEAVY ROD SHARPENED ON THE END TO CHOP HOLES THROUGH THE ICE.

ALMOST ANY FISHING ROD WILL WORK, BUT A SMALL LIGHT-WEIGHT ONE IS BEST FOR WINTER BECAUSE THE FISH SEEM TO BITE MORE DELICATELY IN WINTER AND IT'S HARDER TO NOTICE THE BITES.

ONE OF THE MOST FAVORED METHODS OF WINTER FISHING IS TO USE TIP-UPS. THESE ARE MERELY CROSSES OF STICKS TIED TOGETHER. A BRIGHT RED FLAG IS TIED TO ONE END OF ONE STICK AND THE FISHING LINE (USUALLY A LIGHT-WEIGHT MONOFILAMENT) TO THE OTHER. WHEN THE FISH TAKES THE BAIT HE PULLS ONE END OF THE STICK DOWN AND THE FLAG POPS UP. WITH THIS TYPE OF RIG AN ICE FISHERMAN CAN RIG UP SEVERAL FISHING HOLES, FIND A GOOD LOG FOR A SEAT, BUILD A WARM FIRE AND WATCH FOR ACTION. (CHECK LOCAL GAME LAWS)

THE HOOK ON THE FISHING LINE SHOULD BE SMALL AND THE BAIT SHOULD BE SMALL. WINTER FISH SEEM TO BE SOMEWHAT MORE FINICKY.

SOME FISHERMEN LIKE TO DANGLE A FLASHY SPOON DOWN IN THE WATER, THEN JIG IT UP AND DOWN TO PRODUCE A LITTLE FASTER ACTION.

ICE FISHERMEN USE ALMOST ANY KIND OF BAIT RANGING FROM FISHING WORMS TO MINNOWS.

Marb Gregory

Natural Crafts

ONE EXCELLENT PLACE TO LOOK FOR WINTER ICE FISHING BAIT IS UNDER A PILE OF OLD BOARDS, OR BREAK OPEN AN OLD ROTTEN LOG, YOU'LL FIND LOTS OF FAT GRUBS.

A SECOND SPOT FOR WINTER BAIT IS IN PLANT GALLS SUCH AS ON GOLDENROD PLANTS.

CUT OPEN THE GALLS AND REMOVE THE GRUB.

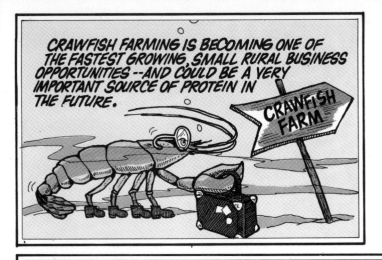

CRAWFISH FARMING IS BECOMING ONE OF THE FASTEST GROWING, SMALL RURAL BUSINESS OPPORTUNITIES --AND COULD BE A VERY IMPORTANT SOURCE OF PROTEIN IN THE FUTURE.

CRAWFISH FARM

NATURAL FOODS

Crawfish New Orleans

- 3 DOZEN CRAWFISH
- 3 TABLESPOONS BUTTER
- 2 SMALL ONIONS
- 3 CELERY STALKS
- 1 TEASPOON SALT
- ½ TEASPOON THYME
- 4 SMALL TOMATOES
- 3 DROPS TABASCO SAUCE
- 1 CUP COOKED RICE

BROWN ONION and CELERY IN BUTTER, ADD SALT AND PEPPER. CUT TOMATO INTO CHUNKS AND ADD. ALLOW MIXTURE TO SIMMER UNTIL TOMATOES ARE SOFT. ADD TABASCO SAUCE, RICE and CRAWFISH. COVER, SIMMER FOR 10 MINUTES.

CRAWFISH ARE A GOURMET'S TREAT. A CLOSE COUSIN OF THE SALT WATER SHRIMP, THEY'RE JUST A BIT MORE DELICATELY FLAVORED and WITH A SOMEWHAT SWEETER TASTE. FOUND IN WATERS ALL OVER THE U.S. AND CANADA FROM HUGE LAKES AND STREAMS TO CITY-PARK PONDS, CRAWFISH ARE ONE SOURCE OF NATURAL FOOD THAT IS IGNORED BY TOO MANY PEOPLE.

THERE ARE SEVERAL WAYS OF CATCHING CRAWFISH.
ONE WAY TO CATCH CRAWFISH FROM STREAMS or LAKES IS TO TIE A SMALL CHUNK OF BACON ONTO A FISH LINE. LOWER THE LINE INTO THE LAKE UNTIL IT TOUCHES BOTTOM. WAIT VERY QUIETLY UNTIL YOU FEEL THE LINE MOVE SLIGHTLY. ALLOW THE "CRAWDAD" TO GET A FIRM GRASP ON THE BAIT, THEN SLOWLY AND CAREFULLY PULL HIM UP. JUST AS HE REACHES THE SURFACE OF THE WATER SLIP A LONG HANDLED MINNOW DIPNET UNDER HIM.

A SECOND METHOD, AND ONE FOR PRODUCING MORE CRAWFISH AT A TIME IS TO SEINE OR NET THEM USING A SMALL MINNOW SEINE (CHECK LOCAL FISH AND GAME LAWS FIRST.). CRAWFISH ARE EASILY CAUGHT IN THIS MANNER FROM SMALL STREAMS OR FROM THE SHALLOWS OF LAKES. IT TAKES TWO PEOPLE TO DO A GOOD JOB OF SEINING, AND YOU SHOULD MAKE SURE THAT THE BOTTOM OF THE SEINE REACHES THE BOTTOM OF THE STREAM OR LAKE EDGE --- OTHERWISE, THE CRAWFISH WILL SLIP UNDER THE SEINE.

CRAWFISH SHOULD FIRST BE "DE-VEINED", THEN BOILED.

1. TO "DE-VEIN" THEM GRASP THE CENTER SEGMENT OF THE TAIL AND PULL WITH A TWISTING MOVEMENT.

2. BOIL FOR ABOUT 10 MINUTES IN SALT WATER.

3. PEEL OFF THE THIN SHELL AND LEGS, THEN CUT OFF THE HEAD AT THE FIRST SEGMENTED JOINT.

THE MEAT MAY THEN BE CHILLED FOR COCKTAILS, SUBSTITUTED FOR ALMOST ANY RECIPE CALLING FOR SHRIMP OR PRAWNS, OR EVEN FROZEN FOR LATER USE.

Mark Gregory

Natural Crafts

ANOTHER WAY OF CATCHING CRAWFISH IS IN A HOME-MADE MINNOW TRAP MADE FROM A QUART FRUIT JAR.

1. PLACE A FUNNEL MADE OF SCREEN WIRE OVER THE MOUTH OF THE FRUIT JAR.

2. PLACE BREAD SCRAPS AND PIECES OF BACON IN THE FRUIT JAR AND LOWER TO BOTTOM OF STREAM OR LAKE.

3. LEAVE OVERNIGHT, THEN CHECK YOUR "CRAWDAD" TRAPS ON THE NEXT MORNING.

DRAINING OF SWAMPS FOR VARIOUS DEVELOPMENT PROJECTS IS ONE OF THE WORST PROBLEMS OUR WILDLIFE FACES TODAY.

SHOPPING CENTER COMING SOON

NATURAL FOODS

CHICKEN FRIED FROG LEGS

SALT AND PEPPER LEGS TO TASTE. BEAT ¼ CUP OF MILK and 2 EGGS TOGETHER, THEN ROLL LEGS IN MIXTURE. COVER LEGS WITH LAYER OF DRY BREAD CRUMBS or CORNMEAL. FRY IN A SKILLET OF SMOKING HOT VEGETABLE OIL. COOK NO LONGER THAN 5 MINUTES, ROLLING THE LEGS TO BROWN THEM ON ALL SIDES.

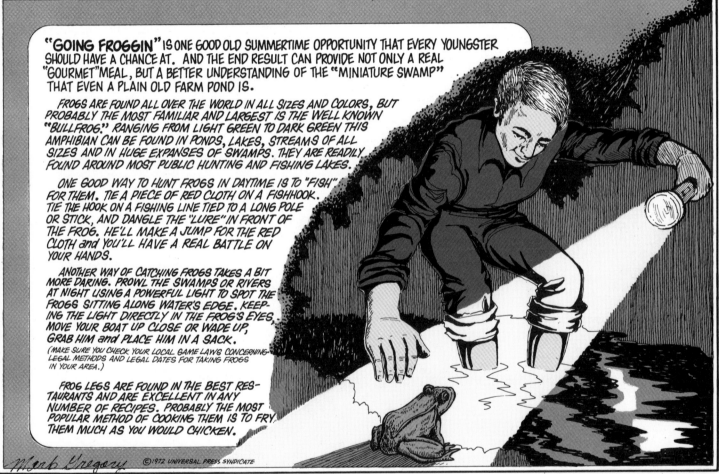

"GOING FROGGIN" IS ONE GOOD OLD SUMMERTIME OPPORTUNITY THAT EVERY YOUNGSTER SHOULD HAVE A CHANCE AT. AND THE END RESULT CAN PROVIDE NOT ONLY A REAL "GOURMET" MEAL, BUT A BETTER UNDERSTANDING OF THE "MINIATURE SWAMP" THAT EVEN A PLAIN OLD FARM POND IS.

FROGS ARE FOUND ALL OVER THE WORLD IN ALL SIZES AND COLORS, BUT PROBABLY THE MOST FAMILIAR AND LARGEST IS THE WELL KNOWN "BULLFROG." RANGING FROM LIGHT GREEN TO DARK GREEN THIS AMPHIBIAN CAN BE FOUND IN PONDS, LAKES, STREAMS OF ALL SIZES AND IN HUGE EXPANSES OF SWAMPS. THEY ARE READILY FOUND AROUND MOST PUBLIC HUNTING AND FISHING LAKES.

ONE GOOD WAY TO HUNT FROGS IN DAYTIME IS TO "FISH" FOR THEM. TIE A PIECE OF RED CLOTH ON A FISHHOOK. TIE THE HOOK ON A FISHING LINE TIED TO A LONG POLE OR STICK, AND DANGLE THE "LURE" IN FRONT OF THE FROG. HE'LL MAKE A JUMP FOR THE RED CLOTH and YOU'LL HAVE A REAL BATTLE ON YOUR HANDS.

ANOTHER WAY OF CATCHING FROGS TAKES A BIT MORE DARING. PROWL THE SWAMPS OR RIVERS AT NIGHT USING A POWERFUL LIGHT TO SPOT THE FROGS SITTING ALONG WATER'S EDGE. KEEPING THE LIGHT DIRECTLY IN THE FROG'S EYES, MOVE YOUR BOAT UP CLOSE OR WADE UP, GRAB HIM and PLACE HIM IN A SACK. (MAKE SURE YOU CHECK YOUR LOCAL GAME LAWS CONCERNING LEGAL METHODS AND LEGAL DATES FOR TAKING FROGS IN YOUR AREA.)

FROG LEGS ARE FOUND IN THE BEST RESTAURANTS AND ARE EXCELLENT IN ANY NUMBER OF RECIPES. PROBABLY THE MOST POPULAR METHOD OF COOKING THEM IS TO FRY THEM MUCH AS YOU WOULD CHICKEN.

Merb Gregory ©1972 UNIVERSAL PRESS SYNDICATE

Natural Crafts

LOOK FOR WATER "GREEN" IS A FAMILIAR ITEM IN YOUR SUPERMARKET AND IS FREE FOR THE PICKING. WHILE YOU'RE FROGGING, CRESS. THIS DELIGHTFUL WILD

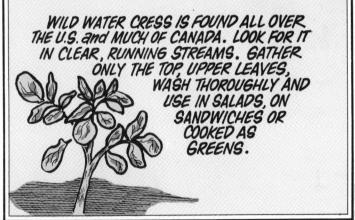

WILD WATER CRESS IS FOUND ALL OVER THE U.S. and MUCH OF CANADA. LOOK FOR IT IN CLEAR, RUNNING STREAMS. GATHER ONLY THE TOP, UPPER LEAVES, WASH THOROUGHLY AND USE IN SALADS, ON SANDWICHES OR COOKED AS GREENS.

THE NUMBER OF FARM PONDS AND MAN-MADE LAKES IS GROWING FAST, AND THEY PROVIDE EXCELLENT TURTLE HABITAT.

SLURP!

NATURAL FOODS

TURTLE SOUP

- 2 CUPS TURTLE MEAT (CUT INTO BITE SIZE PIECES)
- 1 ONION DICED
- 1 CARROT DICED
- 1 LARGE POTATO DICED
- 1 CUP PEAS, TOMATOES or OTHER VEG.
- SALT and PEPPER TO TASTE
- 2 CUPS WATER

SIMMER UNTIL TENDER, THICKEN WITH FLOUR (IF NEC.)

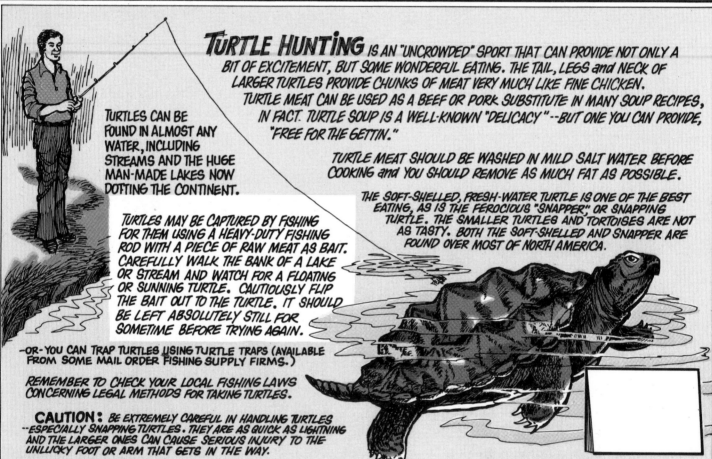

TURTLE HUNTING IS AN "UNCROWDED" SPORT THAT CAN PROVIDE NOT ONLY A BIT OF EXCITEMENT, BUT SOME WONDERFUL EATING. THE TAIL, LEGS and NECK OF LARGER TURTLES PROVIDE CHUNKS OF MEAT VERY MUCH LIKE FINE CHICKEN. TURTLE MEAT CAN BE USED AS A BEEF OR PORK SUBSTITUTE IN MANY SOUP RECIPES, IN FACT. TURTLE SOUP IS A WELL-KNOWN "DELICACY"--BUT ONE YOU CAN PROVIDE, "FREE FOR THE GETTIN'."

TURTLES CAN BE FOUND IN ALMOST ANY WATER, INCLUDING STREAMS AND THE HUGE MAN-MADE LAKES NOW DOTTING THE CONTINENT.

TURTLE MEAT SHOULD BE WASHED IN MILD SALT WATER BEFORE COOKING and YOU SHOULD REMOVE AS MUCH FAT AS POSSIBLE.

THE SOFT-SHELLED, FRESH-WATER TURTLE IS ONE OF THE BEST EATING, AS IS THE FEROCIOUS "SNAPPER" OR SNAPPING TURTLE. THE SMALLER TURTLES AND TORTOISES ARE NOT AS TASTY. BOTH THE SOFT-SHELLED AND SNAPPER ARE FOUND OVER MOST OF NORTH AMERICA.

TURTLES MAY BE CAPTURED BY FISHING FOR THEM USING A HEAVY-DUTY FISHING ROD WITH A PIECE OF RAW MEAT AS BAIT. CAREFULLY WALK THE BANK OF A LAKE OR STREAM AND WATCH FOR A FLOATING OR SUNNING TURTLE. CAUTIOUSLY FLIP THE BAIT OUT TO THE TURTLE. IT SHOULD BE LEFT ABSOLUTELY STILL FOR SOMETIME BEFORE TRYING AGAIN.

–OR-YOU CAN TRAP TURTLES USING TURTLE TRAPS (AVAILABLE FROM SOME MAIL ORDER FISHING SUPPLY FIRMS.)

REMEMBER TO CHECK YOUR LOCAL FISHING LAWS CONCERNING LEGAL METHODS FOR TAKING TURTLES.

CAUTION: BE EXTREMELY CAREFUL IN HANDLING TURTLES --ESPECIALLY SNAPPING TURTLES. THEY ARE AS QUICK AS LIGHTNING AND THE LARGER ONES CAN CAUSE SERIOUS INJURY TO THE UNLUCKY FOOT OR ARM THAT GETS IN THE WAY.

© 1972 UNIVERSAL PRESS SYNDICATE

Mark Gregory

Natural Crafts

TRAPPING TURTLES IS PROBABLY THE MOST PRODUCTIVE METHOD OF CATCHING THEM.

CURRENT

BAIT

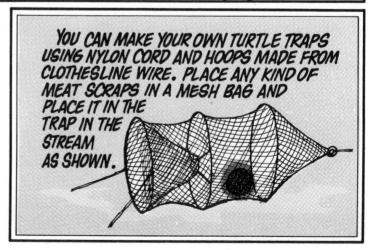

YOU CAN MAKE YOUR OWN TURTLE TRAPS USING NYLON CORD AND HOOPS MADE FROM CLOTHESLINE WIRE. PLACE ANY KIND OF MEAT SCRAPS IN A MESH BAG AND PLACE IT IN THE TRAP IN THE STREAM AS SHOWN.

5
CAMPING

THE BACKPACKER IS HIS OWN FREE MAN, FREE FROM THE "CIVILIZED" PROBLEMS OF AUTOS, NOISE AND "UNFRIENDLY CONCRETE."

NATURAL FOODS

AN EXCELLENT BACKPACKING FOOD IS DRIED FRUIT SUCH AS APRICOTS OR PEACHES. IT CAN BE EATEN WHILE ON THE TRAIL AS AN ENERGY-GIVING SNACK, OR SIMMERED IN WATER FOR A DELICIOUS DESSERT.

APRICOT

TRY **BACKPACKING** AND HIKING FOR A FUN, EDUCATIONAL and ECONOMICAL VACATION. THE BACKPACKER CARRIES HIS HOME ON HIS BACK AND SEES THE OUTDOORS AS IT REALLY IS, NOT FROM A SPEEDING AUTO ON A MONOTONOUS INTERSTATE HIGHWAY. BACKPACKING HAS NO AGE LIMIT BUT DOES REQUIRE GOOD HEALTH AND A GENUINE DESIRE TO DIS-COVER THE "TRUE OUTDOORS."

IF YOU WANT TO TRY BACKPACKING WITHOUT THE EXPENSE OF BUYING ALL THE NECESSARY GEAR, YOU CAN RENT COMPLETE OUTFITS FROM MANY SPORTING GOOD STORES or "OUTFITTERS."

IF YOU WANT TO TRY THIS FUN FAMILY HOBBY, HERE ARE SOME GOOD TIPS FOR THE BEGINNING TRAVELER.

1. START YOUR BACKPACKING TRIPS WITH EASY OVERNIGHT TRIPS.
2. BEFORE YOU START YOUR HIKE, STUDY THE AREA YOU WILL BE HIKING, USING TOPOGRAPHICAL MAPS or OUTDOOR TRAIL GUIDES (AVAILABLE AT LOCAL BOOK STORES).
3. SELECTING FOOD IS NO PROBLEM EVEN FOR THE BEGINNER. MOST CAMPING and SPORTING GOODS STORES STOCK COMPLETE MEALS OF "FREEZE-DRIED" FOODS. SELECT THE PRE-PORTIONED MEALS YOU DESIRE.
4. DON'T TRY TO PACK MORE THAN YOU CAN SAFELY CARRY. HEALTHY ADULTS SHOULD START WITH ABOUT 35 POUNDS. YOUNGSTERS UNDER 15 SHOULD CARRY LESS THAN 25 POUNDS.
5. WEAR LOOSE FITTING, COMFORTABLE CLOTHING and, MOST OF ALL, _GOOD HIKING BOOTS_.
6. MAKE A CHECKLIST BEFORE YOU LEAVE, AND MAKE SURE YOU HAVE EVERYTHING YOU NEED.
7. PACK HEAVY ITEMS IN BAG AS HIGH and CLOSE TO YOUR BODY AS POSSIBLE. PACK LIGHTWEIGHT ITEMS ON BOTTOM.
8. PACK OUT EVERYTHING YOU PACK IN.
9. KEEP COOKING and HEATING FIRES TO A MINIMUM and MAKE SURE THEY'RE OUT BEFORE YOU LEAVE.

© 1972 Universal Press Syndicate

CHECK LIST: ⟍KNIFE ⟍ROPE ⟍SNAKE BITE KIT ⟍FIRST AID KIT ⟍REPAIR KIT ⟍PACK and FRAME ⟍SUNGLASSES ⟍TENT LIGHTWEIGHT MOUNTAIN STYLE ⟍PERSONAL TOILET KIT ⟍SUNBURN LOTION ⟍SOAP ⟍SLEEPING BAG DOWN FILLED ⟍SAFETY PINS ⟍CANDLES ⟍PONCHO ⟍CANTEEN ⟍FOAM or AIR MATTRESS ⟍COMPASS ⟍FOOD ⟍EXTRA CLOTHING ⟍MAP ⟍COOKING GEAR ⟍TOILET PAPER ⟍SCOURING PADS ⟍MATCHES ⟍HATCHET ⟍SMALL TOWEL ⟍MOSQUITO REPELLENT

WHERE TO GO: CHECK WITH YOUR LOCAL STATE or PROVINCE TOURISM COMMISSION FOR BACKPACKING TRAILS IN YOUR AREA. FOR GUIDED HIKING and BACKPACKING TRIPS WRITE TO: Sierra Club, Mills Tower, San Francisco, Cal. 94104, or to American Youth Hostels, 535 West End Av., New York, NY 10024.

Mack Gregory

Natural Crafts

THE BEST FIRE STARTER IS A CANDLE. IT WILL LAST LONGER THAN ANY MATCH AND WON'T GO OUT WHEN DAMP.

ALWAYS CARRY WATERPROOFED MATCHES IN A WATERPROOF MATCH CASE WHEN HIKING OR BACKPACKING.

A GOOD DOUBLE-BITTED **AXE** IS A BASIC TOOL OF SURVIVAL.

A GOOD NATURAL *COUGH SYRUP* CAN BE MADE BY BOILING THE JUICE OF A LEMON FOR 10 MINUTES, THEN MIXING WITH A CUP OF HONEY. STIR THOROUGHLY BEFORE USING. GIVE AS NEEDED.

USING AN AXE IS ESSENTIAL TO OUTDOORSMEN AND CAMPERS, BUT IT IS ALSO EXCELLENT EXERCISE, AND WILL BUILD UP YOUR WIND, ENDURANCE AND COORDINATION -- NOT TO SPEAK OF A SUPPLY OF KINDLING FOR COLD WINTER NIGHTS.

THE FIRST RULE IN AXEMANSHIP IS THAT **THE BLADE MUST BE SHARP.** A DULL BLADE WILL CAUSE THE AXE HEAD TO GLANCE -- *POSSIBLY CAUSING INJURY.* USING A GOOD MILL FILE (AVAILABLE AT HARDWARE STORES), SHARPEN THE AXE EDGE THOROUGHLY BEFORE USING IT.

THE SECOND RULE IS TO MAKE SURE THE AREA AROUND YOU IS **CLEAR** AND FREE OF OVERHANGING TREE LIMBS, *etc.,* AND THAT THERE IS NOTHING ON THE GROUND YOU MAY STUMBLE OR FALL OVER.

THE THIRD RULE IS TO SET A **RHYTHM**. ALLOW THE AXE TO WORK FOR YOU, SWING IT DOWN INTO THE WOOD, PULL IT BACK OFF, SWING IT BACK UP BEHIND YOU AND ALLOW IT TO FALL OF ITS OWN ACCORD, GUIDING IT AND APPLYING ONLY LIGHT PRESSURE.

ALWAYS TRY TO MAKE YOUR CUTS AT A SHARP ANGLE INTO THE WOOD. THIS SLICES CLEANLY AND MUCH DEEPER THAN IN COMING DOWN STRAIGHT AT THE LOG.

WHEN FELLING TREES, FIRST MAKE A V-CUT OVER HALF THE THICKNESS OF THE TREE. MAKE A SECOND V-CUT FROM THE OPPOSITE SIDE OF THE TREE, AND THE TREE WILL TEND TO FALL IN THE DIRECTION OF THE FIRST V-CUT.

TO "BUCK" OR CUT LIMBS OFF THE TREE, STAND TO ONE SIDE AND CHOP ON THE OPPOSITE SIDE, LOPPING OFF THE BRANCHES FROM THE BUTT END OF THE TREE TOWARD THE TOP. MAKE SURE THE TREE WON'T ROLL ON YOU WHEN YOU CUT OFF SOME OF THE BRANCHES.

WHEN CHOPPING LARGER BRANCHES AND LOGS INTO PIECES, SPREAD YOUR FEET WIDE FOR BALANCE, AND STAND ON THE OPPOSITE SIDE FROM THAT YOU'RE CHOPPING ON.

TO SPLIT LOGS LAY THEM IN A CROTCH OF A TREE OR STAND THEM ON END. DON'T ATTEMPT TO SPLIT LOGS LYING ON THE GROUND -- *THEY WILL ROLL, CAUSING THE AXE TO GLANCE.*

TO CUT SMALL STICKS, PLACE THEM ON A CHOPPING BLOCK OR LARGE LOG. *DON'T CUT THEM WHILE THEY ARE LYING ON THE GROUND -- THE ENDS MAY FLY UP.*

WHEN YOU'RE CUTTING SMALL SAPLINGS, BEND THEM OVER AS CLOSE TO THE GROUND AS POSSIBLE, THEN CUT THEM OFF CLOSE TO THE GROUND.

Natural Crafts

SPLITTING FIREWOOD LOGS CAN BE DONE WITH A "FAT" WEDGE-SHAPED AXE, OR WITH METAL WEDGES AND A MALLET. IF THERE IS MUCH WOOD TO BE CUT, DO AS THE OLD TIMERS DID AND SPLIT IT WITH WEDGES AND A MALLET.

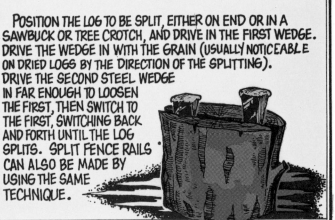

POSITION THE LOG TO BE SPLIT, EITHER ON END OR IN A SAWBUCK OR TREE CROTCH, AND DRIVE IN THE FIRST WEDGE. DRIVE THE WEDGE IN WITH THE GRAIN (USUALLY NOTICEABLE ON DRIED LOGS BY THE DIRECTION OF THE SPLITTING). DRIVE THE SECOND STEEL WEDGE IN FAR ENOUGH TO LOOSEN THE FIRST, THEN SWITCH TO THE FIRST, SWITCHING BACK AND FORTH UNTIL THE LOG SPLITS. SPLIT FENCE RAILS CAN ALSO BE MADE BY USING THE SAME TECHNIQUE.

A WARM, COZY CAMPFIRE FLICKERING IN A STARLIT NIGHT PROVIDES THOSE MOMENTS OF SELF-REFLECTION THAT ARE VITAL TO MAN'S SPIRIT.

NATURAL FOODS

TRY MAKING YOUR NEXT OUTDOOR COFFEE THE OLD-TIME WAY. MERELY PLACE A HANDFULL OF REGULAR GRIND COFFEE IN A CAN OF COLD WATER (called a "billy" by trappers). BRING THE WATER TO A BOIL AND ALLOW IT TO BREW UNTIL THE COFFEE REACHES THE RIGHT COLOR FOR YOUR TASTE. THROW IN A TEASPOON OF COLD WATER AND ALLOW THE GROUNDS TO SETTLE TO THE BOTTOM. DELICIOUS!

KNOWING THE BASICS OF MAKING A SAFE AND PROPER FIRE IS ESSENTIAL WHETHER YOU'RE AT HOME WITH YOUR OWN COZY FIREPLACE, OR STOPPING FOR TEA AND A TRAIL LUNCH DEEP IN THE WILDERNESS. TEACHING A YOUNGSTER HOW TO QUICKLY BUILD A SAFE AND PROPER FIRE IS AS IMPORTANT AS TEACHING HIM TO SWIM.

A FIRE CONSISTS OF THREE ITEMS: TINDER (fire starter), KINDLING OR TINY PIECES OF EASILY BURNED WOOD, AND MEDIUM SIZE PIECES OF FIREWOOD. THE QUICKEST AND EASIEST WAY TO START A FIRE IS TO PLACE THE KINDLING AROUND THE TINDER, THEN A FEW MEDIUM SIZE PIECES OF WOOD AROUND THE KINDLING, ALL SHAPED LIKE A SHOCK OF CORN -- THEN LIGHT THE TINDER.

NATURAL TINDER CAN BE ALMOST ANY EASILY BURNED MATERIAL SUCH AS PINE CONES, SHREDDED CEDAR BARK, DEAD EVERGREEN TWIGS and NEEDLES, and DEAD GRASS. DEAD ROOTS and BRANCHES OF ALMOST ALL EVER-GREENS CONTAIN PITCH AND BURN QUITE READILY.

YOU CAN ALSO MAKE TINDER IN THE FORM OF FUZZ STICKS, A THIN BRANCH THAT HAS BEEN SHAVED WITH A SHARP KNIFE TO PRODUCE THIN SHAVINGS - ALL ATTACHED TO THE BRANCH.

Fuzz Stick

© 1972 Universal Press Syndicate

DIFFERENT SPECIES OF WOODS BURN DIFFERENTLY. AS A RULE, HARDWOODS BURN WITH A HOTTER FLAME, WILL LAST LONGER AND WILL PRODUCE A BETTER BED OF COALS THAN SOFTWOODS. EVERGREENS BURN WELL, BUT HAVE A TENDENCY TO POP AND SPUTTER. MOST SOFTWOODS ARE ALSO SOOTY.

SOME GOOD FIREWOODS ARE: OAK, HICKORY, BIRCH, APPLE, MAPLE, ASH, DOGWOOD, LOCUST, AND MOUNTAIN MAHOGANY.

WARNING: ALWAYS MAKE YOUR FIRES FROM DEAD STANDING TIMBER, AND IF YOU'RE ON PUBLIC PROPERTY, BE SURE IT IS LAWFUL TO CUT TREES, EVEN DEAD ONES.

SAFETY RULES FOR CAMPFIRES --

1. BUILD A FIRE NO LARGER THAN NECESSARY.
2. CLEAR FIRE AREA DOWN TO SOLID DAMP GROUND OF ANY COMBUSTIBLE MATERIAL --DRY LEAVES, ETC. FOR AT LEAST 10 FT. AROUND CAMPFIRE.
3. BE CAREFUL OF HIGH WINDS.
4. DO NOT BUILD FIRES UNDER LOW TREE LIMBS.
5. DO NOT LEAVE FIRES UNATTENDED.
6. ALWAYS KEEP WATER ON HAND TO EXTINGUISH FIRE.
7. MAKE SURE FIRE COALS ARE RAKED APART AND FIRE IS COMPLETELY OUT BEFORE LEAVING CAMP.

Natural Crafts

BUILDING A COOKING CAMPFIRE IS AN ART THAT IS EASILY LEARNED. THE SIMPLEST COOKING FIRE IS A ROW OF LARGE ROCKS PLACED IN A "U" AND JUST FAR ENOUGH APART TO HOLD YOUR COOKING PANS. (Don't use wet rocks from a stream or lake -- they can explode from steam.) OR YOU CAN USE A COUPLE OF LARGE GREEN LOGS FOR THIS TYPE "FIREPLACE." THE OPEN END OF THE CAMPFIRE SHOULD FACE INTO THE WIND TO PROVIDE A DRAFT.

wind

A FAVORITE TRAIL CAMPFIRE FOR INDIANS AND FRONTIERSMEN WHEN TRAVELING LIGHT WAS A SMALL "TEPEE" TYPE FIRE WITH THE FOOD SUSPENDED ON A "DINGLE STICK" OVER THE FIRE. THIS WAS A GREEN SAPLING STUCK INTO THE GROUND AT AN ANGLE AND HANGING OVER THE FIRE. ON IT WAS PLACED ANYTHING FROM BANNOCK (BREAD) TO A PIECE OF RABBIT OR FISH.

SNOW SHOES MAKE WINTER CAMPING EASIER IN SOME PARTS OF THE COUNTRY, OR TRY SKIS IF YOU'RE EXPERIENCED.

NATURAL FOODS

EAT A HIGH-ENERGY SNACK BEFORE GOING TO BED AND YOU'LL STAY WARM EASIER.

IF YOU'RE TIRED OF CRAMPED, NOISY "OUTDOOR GHETTO" CAMPING, TRY COLD-WEATHER CAMPING. EVEN PARKS AND CAMPGROUNDS THAT ARE THE MOST CROWDED IN SUMMER TAKE ON A NEW LOOK AND A SPECIAL "LONELINESS" IN WINTER.

AND IF YOU'RE AN EXPERIENCED CAMPER TRY SOME BACK-COUNTRY WINTER CAMPING. WITH THE PROPER KNOW-HOW AND EQUIPMENT THIS CAN BE A BEAUTIFUL EXPERIENCE.

WINTER CAMPING IS NO MORE DANGEROUS THAN SUMMER CAMPING, BUT DOES REQUIRE SPECIAL EQUIPMENT AND ATTENTION TO SOME NEW RULES.

1. WEARING THE PROPER CLOTHING IS OF EXTREME IMPORTANCE IN COLD-WEATHER CAMPING. YOUR CLOTHING MUST HOLD IN BODY HEAT YET ALLOW PERSPIRATION TO EVAPORATE AWAY FROM YOUR BODY. EVEN A LITTLE PERSPIRATION CAN BE DANGEROUS IN EXTREME COLD TEMPERATURES. WEAR SEVERAL LAYERS OF CLOTHING AND REMOVE AS NEEDED WHEN YOU'RE HIKING OR WORKING, THEN REPLACE WHEN YOU STOP. WOOL HAS BEEN A FAVORITE FOR MANY YEARS AS A COLD-WEATHER CLOTHING. MANY PEOPLE, HOWEVER, CAN'T WEAR WOOL UNDERWEAR, AND THE NEW "FISH-NET" UNDERWEAR WILL SERVE THE SAME PURPOSE. IN EXTREMELY COLD AND WINDY WEATHER, WHEN THE WIND-CHILL FACTOR MAY BE EXTREMELY LOW, WEAR A WIND-PROOF PARKA. WEAR WATERPROOF BOOTS WITH AT LEAST TWO PAIRS OF WOOL SOCKS. AS FOR HEADGEAR, I LIKE A WOOL SEA CAP THAT CAN BE PULLED DOWN OVER MY EARS, THEN A PARKA HOOD OVER THAT FOR COLD WEATHER.

2. THE NEXT ESSENTIAL IS A GOOD SLEEPING BAG. CHOOSE ONE RATED FOR SUB-ZERO WEATHER (AT LEAST A 4-POUND BAG) PREFERABLY MADE OF GOOSE DOWN. USE PLENTY OF INSULATION UNDER YOUR SLEEPING BAG, EITHER A GOOD FOAM RUBBER PAD OR EVERGREEN BOUGHS.

3. TAKE A TENT THAT CAN BE SET UP WITHOUT HAVING TO DRIVE TENT PEGS IN THE FROZEN GROUND, OR LAY LOGS AROUND THE TENT BOTTOM TO HOLD IT IN PLACE.

4. MAKE SURE YOU HAVE A GOOD AXE OR CAMP SAW AND PLENTY OF WATERPROOF MATCHES. KEEP PLENTY OF FIREWOOD ON HAND. CUT SOME EACH NIGHT AND STORE IN YOUR TENT TO MAKE SURE YOU HAVE DRY WOOD FOR STARTING THE MORNING FIRE.

5. DON'T PITCH YOUR TENT UNDER SNOW OR ICE COVERED TREES AND DON'T CAMP IN THE VALLEYS BECAUSE COLD AIR SETTLES IN THE LOWER AREAS AT NIGHT.

6. CARRY PLENTY OF FOOD, ESPECIALLY HIGH-CALORIE AND HIGH-ENERGY FOODS BECAUSE YOU'LL BURN UP A LOT OF ENERGY IN COLD WEATHER JUST STAYING WARM.

7. CHECK WITH YOUR LOCAL CONSERVATION AGENT OR PARK RANGER FOR AREAS OPEN AND SAFE FOR WINTER CAMPING. ALWAYS TELL HIM OR SOMEONE ELSE WHERE YOU'RE GOING AND HOW LONG YOU EXPECT TO BE.

DO NOT BURN CATALYTIC HEATERS OR OTHER TENT HEATERS IN A CLOSED UP TENT. THEY GIVE OFF POISONOUS CARBON MONOXIDE. THE SAME IS TRUE OF CHARCOAL FIRES.

© 1972 UNIVERSAL PRESS SYNDICATE

Marb Gregory

Natural Crafts

ONE OF THE MOST EFFECTIVE TENTS FOR WINTER IS THE OLD-FASHIONED, OPEN-FRONT BAKER TENT.

A REFLECTOR FIRE BUILT IN FRONT WILL KEEP THE TENT COZY ALL NIGHT.

ANOTHER TRICK IS TO BANK SNOW AROUND THE EDGES OF THE TENT. THIS HELPS KEEP OUT THE WIND AND KEEPS HEAT IN THE TENT.

CRACK BOOM

THE WOODSMAN LEARNS TO LIVE WITH NATURE.

NATURAL FOODS

CHOCOLATE SQUARES ARE ONE OF THE BEST SURVIVAL FOODS BECAUSE OF THEIR HIGH ENERGY.

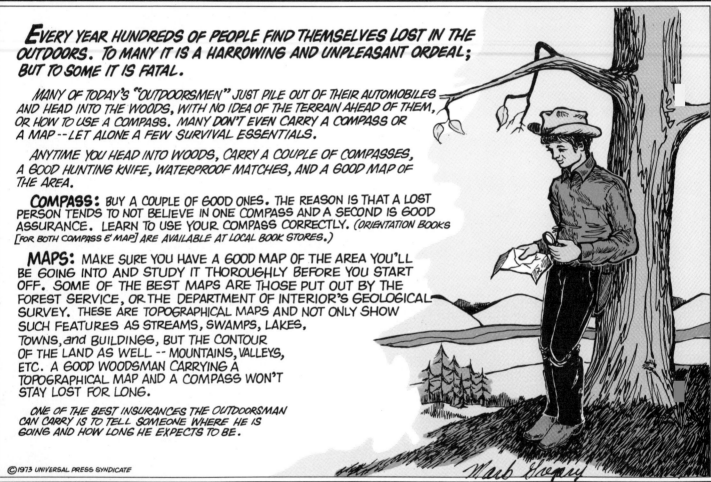

EVERY YEAR HUNDREDS OF PEOPLE FIND THEMSELVES LOST IN THE OUTDOORS. TO MANY IT IS A HARROWING AND UNPLEASANT ORDEAL; BUT TO SOME IT IS FATAL.

MANY OF TODAY'S "OUTDOORSMEN" JUST PILE OUT OF THEIR AUTOMOBILES AND HEAD INTO THE WOODS, WITH NO IDEA OF THE TERRAIN AHEAD OF THEM, OR HOW TO USE A COMPASS. MANY DON'T EVEN CARRY A COMPASS OR A MAP -- LET ALONE A FEW SURVIVAL ESSENTIALS.

ANYTIME YOU HEAD INTO WOODS, CARRY A COUPLE OF COMPASSES, A GOOD HUNTING KNIFE, WATERPROOF MATCHES, AND A GOOD MAP OF THE AREA.

COMPASS: BUY A COUPLE OF GOOD ONES. THE REASON IS THAT A LOST PERSON TENDS TO NOT BELIEVE IN ONE COMPASS AND A SECOND IS GOOD ASSURANCE. LEARN TO USE YOUR COMPASS CORRECTLY. (ORIENTATION BOOKS [FOR BOTH COMPASS & MAP] ARE AVAILABLE AT LOCAL BOOK STORES.)

MAPS: MAKE SURE YOU HAVE A GOOD MAP OF THE AREA YOU'LL BE GOING INTO AND STUDY IT THOROUGHLY BEFORE YOU START OFF. SOME OF THE BEST MAPS ARE THOSE PUT OUT BY THE FOREST SERVICE, OR THE DEPARTMENT OF INTERIOR'S GEOLOGICAL SURVEY. THESE ARE TOPOGRAPHICAL MAPS AND NOT ONLY SHOW SUCH FEATURES AS STREAMS, SWAMPS, LAKES, TOWNS, and BUILDINGS, BUT THE CONTOUR OF THE LAND AS WELL -- MOUNTAINS, VALLEYS, ETC. A GOOD WOODSMAN CARRYING A TOPOGRAPHICAL MAP AND A COMPASS WON'T STAY LOST FOR LONG.

ONE OF THE BEST INSURANCES THE OUTDOORSMAN CAN CARRY IS TO TELL SOMEONE WHERE HE IS GOING AND HOW LONG HE EXPECTS TO BE.

Mark Gregory

Natural Crafts

EXPERIENCED WOODSMEN CARRY A TINY SURVIVAL KIT WITH THEM AT ALL TIMES -- EVEN WHEN GOING INTO WOODS THEY KNOW THOROUGHLY.

SURVIVAL KIT

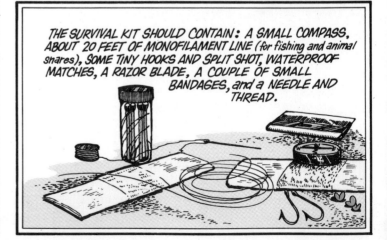

THE SURVIVAL KIT SHOULD CONTAIN: A SMALL COMPASS, ABOUT 20 FEET OF MONOFILAMENT LINE (for fishing and animal snares), SOME TINY HOOKS AND SPLIT SHOT, WATERPROOF MATCHES, A RAZOR BLADE, A COUPLE OF SMALL BANDAGES, and a NEEDLE AND THREAD.

THE EARLY WOODSMAN'S SURVIVAL DEPENDED UPON HIS KEEN "SENSES."

ONE SURE SIGN OF BAD WEATHER IN THE FALL IS A LARGE NUMBER OF WATERFOWL MOVING SOUTH.

THE OLD-TIME WOODSMEN WERE EXPERTS AT FORE-CASTING WEATHER BY OBSERVING NATURAL SIGNS. THEY HAD TO BE; OFTEN TIMES THEIR LIVES DEPENDED ON WEATHER CONDITIONS. ANYONE WHO SPENDS A LITTLE TIME OUTDOORS CAN EASILY LEARN TO UTILIZE THESE OBSERVATIONS.

1. ONE OF THE EASIEST TO RECOGNIZE, AND MOST POPULAR PREDICTIONS OF A STORM MOVING IN, IS THE LEAVES OF DECIDUOUS TREES TURNING BOTTOM SIDE UP, OR AS THE OLD TIMERS SAY, "WHEN THE LEAVES SHOW THEIR UNDERSIDES." THIS USUALLY HAPPENS FROM 12 TO 24 HOURS BEFORE A STORM.

2. THE ANTS WERE A FAVORITE PREDICTOR OF AN UNCLE OF MINE. WHEN THE ANTS START BUILDING MOUNDS OR TINY "DIKES" AROUND THE ENTRANCE TO THEIR TUNNELS, WATCH FOR RAIN. ALL ACTIVITY WILL USUALLY STOP AT LEAST AN HOUR BEFORE THE STORM IS DUE TO HIT.

3. ALL ANIMALS ARE MORE ACTIVE IN THE 24-HOUR PERIOD BEFORE A STORM. THE LARGER ANIMALS SUCH AS DEER OR MOOSE FEED HEAVILY WHILE THE SMALLER ANIMALS SUCH AS MICE SCURRY TO HIGHER GROUND. ALL ACTIVITY WILL USUALLY STOP JUST BEFORE THE STORM BEGINS.

4. A STILL MORNING WITH LOTS OF DEW OR FROST ON THE GRASS USUALLY PREDICTS A CLEAR DAY, BUT A DRY MORNING USUALLY MEANS RAIN IS MOVING IN.

5. AN UNUSUAL NUMBER OF HAWKS CIRCLING THE AIR OR PERCHING IN THE HIGH "LOOK-OUTS" OF THE TREE TOPS INDICATES A STORM MOVING IN. THE HAWKS ARE WATCHING THE INCREASED ACTIVITY OF THE MICE, TOADS AND TURTLES AS THEY MOVE AROUND, CROSSING OPEN AREAS.

ANT HILL

Mark Gregory

Natural Crafts

SMOKE THAT RISES STRAIGHT UP FROM THE CAMPFIRE PREDICTS CLEAR WEATHER. SMOKE HANGING IN LOW TO THE GROUND INDICATES A STORM BREWING.

THE OLD SAILOR'S CHANT: RED SKY IN THE MORNING--SAILORS TAKE WARNING; RED SKY AT NIGHT--SAILORS' DELIGHT, IS AN OLD-TIME THEORY THAT SEEMS TO WORK.

TAKE A LOOK AT YOUR SURROUNDINGS!

CAN <u>YOU</u> IMPROVE

OUR WILDLIFE HABITAT

?

Soybeans ARE PROBABLY THE WORLD'S OLDEST FOOD CROP AND THERE ARE LITERALLY HUNDREDS OF WAYS TO PREPARE THIS NUTRITIONAL FOOD.

For instance they may be cooked in pods as green beans, or used as Soy milk, a substitute for cows' milk (available at natural food stores). Soybeans have more concentrated nutrition than almost any other plant.

ONE OF THE MOST VALUABLE FOODS OF THE AMERICAN INDIAN WAS "JERKY" WHICH HE MADE FROM VENISON, BUFFALO, ELK, ETC. HE DEVELOPED THIS METHOD OF PRESERVING MEAT BECAUSE OF NECESSITY. IN FACT, INDIANS OF THE NORTHERN COUNTRY (ALASKA, YUKON) STILL PRESERVE MEAT IN THIS SAME WAY. IT'S EASY, FUN AND A GREAT WAY OF PREPARING A "SNACK" YOU CAN EASILY CARRY WITH YOU ON HIKES OR BACK-PACKING TRIPS.

JERKY CAN BE MADE OF ALMOST ANY MEAT FROM BEEF to VENISON to PORK. HOWEVER, IF YOU USE WILD MEAT OR PORK, YOU MUST BOIL THE MEAT SLICES JUST LONG ENOUGH TO REMOVE THE RED TO INSURE AGAINST TRICHINA *(A PARASITE COMMON IN MANY WILD ANIMALS)*.

Step 1. SLICE THE MEAT INTO 1/8 to 1/4 INCH STRIPS WITH THE GRAIN AND REMOVE ALL FAT. *AVOID EXTRA TOUGH MEATS.*

Step 2. MARINATE THE STRIPS OVERNIGHT IN A SOLUTION OF SALT, PEPPER, ONION, GARLIC AND WORCHESTERSHIRE OR TOBASCO SAUCE IF YOU WANT HOT, SPICY JERKY.

recipe
1 tablespoon Salt
1 tablespoon Onion powder
1 teaspoon Garlic powder
1/2 teaspoon Pepper
Enough water to cover meat.

Step 3. DRAIN MARINATED STRIPS ON TOWELLING.

Step 4. PLACE ON THE WIRE RACKS OF YOUR OVEN SO THAT NO STRIPS ARE TOUCHING OR OVERLAPPING. BAKE AT LOWEST POSSIBLE HEAT (WARM OR 200°) WITH THE OVEN DOOR PROPPED SLIGHTLY OPEN FOR 2 TO 3 HOURS - OR UNTIL THE STRIPS ARE COAL BLACK AND CRACK WHEN BENT BUT DO NOT BREAK. YOU SHOULD PLACE A COOKIE SHEET OR FOIL IN THE BOTTOM OF THE OVEN TO CATCH DRIPS.

Your Jerky CAN USUALLY BE KEPT IN SEALED PLASTIC BAGS OR JARS FOR AT LEAST A YEAR WITHOUT REFRIGERATION. TO CARRY JERKY ON LONG BACK-PACK TRIPS, PLACE THE PLASTIC BAGS INSIDE CLOTH BAGS TO PROTECT THE PLASTIC FROM TEARS.

© 1972 UNIVERSAL PRESS SYNDICATE

YOU CAN ALSO MAKE JERKY OUTSIDE

IN EXACTLY THE SAME WAY THE INDIANS DID. TWO METHODS WERE USED. IN HOT, DRY CLIMATES, THE PREPARED STRIPS OF MEAT WERE SIMPLY LAID OUT ON WOODEN RACKS TO DRY IN THE HOT SUN. IF YOU FOLLOW THIS METHOD, YOU SHOULD PROVIDE PROTECTION FROM INSECTS. COVER AT NIGHT TO KEEP MEAT DRY.

A SMALL SMOKER WAS ALSO USED.

BUILT OF ANIMAL SKINS AND SHAPED LIKE A MINIATURE TEPEE, IT HAD RACKS FOR THE MEAT AT ITS TOP AND A TINY "SMUDGE" OR SMOKE FIRE BUILT UNDER IT. THE FIRE WAS NOT ALLOWED TO GET HOT ENOUGH TO COOK THE MEAT-- BUT ONLY TO SLOWLY DRY IT OUT. A MODERNIZED VERSION CAN BE MADE FROM A CLEANED OIL DRUM. USE HICKORY WOOD CHIPS FOR THE SMUDGE FIRE.

AIR HOLES

RODS TO HOLD STRIPS

WHEN AN INDIAN HUNTER WENT ON A HUNT, HE TRAVELED AS LIGHT AS POSSIBLE, CARRYING ONLY JERKY or PEMMICAN AS FOOD and FORAGING ON NATURAL FOOD AS HE WENT.

NATURAL FOODS

AN EXCELLENT CAMP STEW CAN BE MADE BY JUST ADDING FLOUR and WATER TO PEMMICAN AND SLOWLY SIMMERING IT.

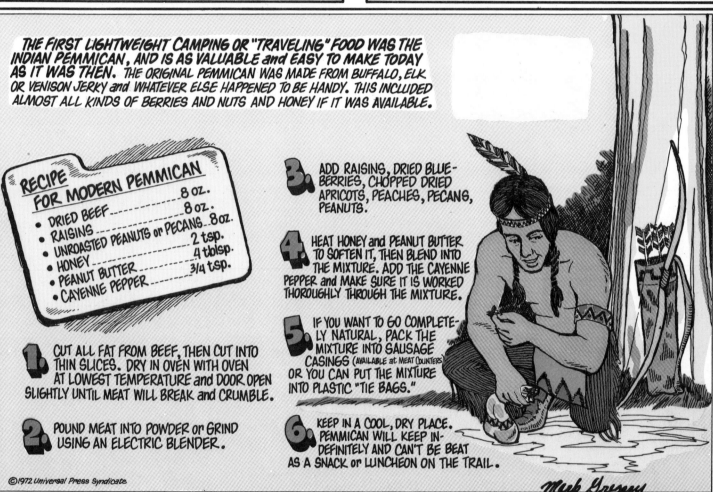

THE FIRST LIGHTWEIGHT CAMPING OR "TRAVELING" FOOD WAS THE INDIAN PEMMICAN, AND IS AS VALUABLE and EASY TO MAKE TODAY AS IT WAS THEN. THE ORIGINAL PEMMICAN WAS MADE FROM BUFFALO, ELK OR VENISON JERKY and WHATEVER ELSE HAPPENED TO BE HANDY. THIS INCLUDED ALMOST ALL KINDS OF BERRIES AND NUTS AND HONEY IF IT WAS AVAILABLE.

RECIPE FOR MODERN PEMMICAN

- DRIED BEEF ———————— 8 oz.
- RAISINS ———————————— 8 oz.
- UNROASTED PEANUTS or PECANS — 8 oz.
- HONEY ———————————— 2 tsp.
- PEANUT BUTTER ————— 4 tblsp.
- CAYENNE PEPPER ———— 3/4 tsp.

1. CUT ALL FAT FROM BEEF, THEN CUT INTO THIN SLICES. DRY IN OVEN WITH OVEN AT LOWEST TEMPERATURE and DOOR OPEN SLIGHTLY UNTIL MEAT WILL BREAK and CRUMBLE.

2. POUND MEAT INTO POWDER or GRIND USING AN ELECTRIC BLENDER.

3. ADD RAISINS, DRIED BLUEBERRIES, CHOPPED DRIED APRICOTS, PEACHES, PECANS, PEANUTS.

4. HEAT HONEY and PEANUT BUTTER TO SOFTEN IT, THEN BLEND INTO THE MIXTURE. ADD THE CAYENNE PEPPER AND MAKE SURE IT IS WORKED THOROUGHLY THROUGH THE MIXTURE.

5. IF YOU WANT TO GO COMPLETELY NATURAL, PACK THE MIXTURE INTO SAUSAGE CASINGS (AVAILABLE at MEAT COUNTERS) OR YOU CAN PUT THE MIXTURE INTO PLASTIC "TIE BAGS."

6. KEEP IN A COOL, DRY PLACE. PEMMICAN WILL KEEP INDEFINITELY AND CAN'T BE BEAT AS A SNACK or LUNCHEON ON THE TRAIL.

©1972 Universal Press Syndicate

Merb Gregory

Natural Crafts

EXCELLENT FOOD CARRYING BAGS FOR BACKPACKERS, CANOERS and OTHER CAMPERS CAN BE MADE FROM DISCARDED LEATHER or SUEDE JACKETS or COATS.

1. CUT MATERIAL INTO 12-INCH CIRCLE.

2. CUT SLITS AROUND OUTSIDE EDGE OF CIRCLE.

3. THREAD LEATHER SHOE LACE THROUGH SLITS, GATHER MATERIAL INTO POUCH.

4. FOR ADDED PROTECTION, USE PLASTIC "TIE BAGS" INSIDE LEATHER POUCH.

LEARN SOME OF THE OLD-TIME WAYS: THEY WERE A MORE NATURAL WAY OF LIFE.

NATURAL FOODS

A FAVORITE FARM SOUP IS CREAM-TOMATO MADE WITH JUST A LITTLE BAKING SODA. YOU CAN MAKE IT IN THE QUANTITIES YOU NEED. POUR MILK IN A SAUCE-PAN. ADD TOMATO SAUCE IN QUANTITY YOU DESIRE FOR TASTE IN PROPORTION TO THE MILK. THEN ADD A PINCH OF BAKING SODA. PUT IN A PAT OF BUTTER IF THE MILK IS SKIM-MILK. SALT AND PEPPER TO TASTE AND SLOWLY HEAT TO A BOIL AND SERVE.

ONE OF THE OUTDOORSMAN'S BEST FRIENDS IS "PLAIN, OLD KITCHEN BAKING SODA," ALSO CALLED BICARBONATE OF SODA. MAKE SURE YOU HAVE PLENTY OF THIS ON HAND FOR YOUR NEXT CAMPING TRIP.

1. SODA MAKES A GOOD EMERGENCY FIRST-AID TREATMENT FOR MANY THINGS. IF YOU RECEIVE A BAD INSECT BITE, MIX A LITTLE SODA WITH WATER TO FORM A PASTE AND KEEP THE PASTE ON THE BITE. THIS ALSO GOES FOR A MINOR BURN (A SUPERFICIAL SKIN BURN ONLY). IF YOU KEEP A WET SOLUTION OF BAKING SODA AND WATER ON THE BURN, IT WILL HELP KEEP THE PAIN DOWN.

THE OLD-TIMERS ALSO KNEW BAKING SODA TO BE A "MEDICINE CHEST IN A BOX." MIXED HALF-AND-HALF WITH SALT IT WAS USED AS A TOOTH PASTE. ADDING THE MIXTURE TO A LITTLE WARM WATER MADE AN EXCELLENT MOUTH WASH. ANOTHER OLD-TIME REMEDY WAS FOR ACID INDIGESTION, AND WAS A HALF TEASPOON OF SODA DISSOLVED IN A GLASS OF WATER.

AN OLD-TIME REMEDY THAT WAS FAVORED BY MY GRANDFATHER, FOR TIRED, ACHING FEET, WAS SOAKING THEM IN A PAN OF WARM "SODY WATER," OR WATER MIXED WITH A COUPLE OF TEASPOONS OF BAKING SODA.

2. A TEASPOON OF BAKING SODA IN A LITTLE WATER POURED INTO A CAMP COOLER OR VACUUM BOTTLE AND LEFT OVER-NIGHT WILL FRESHEN IT.

3. CAMP DISHES, POTS AND PANS CAN ALSO BE EASILY CLEANED BY SOAKING IN A LITTLE WARM WATER CONTAINING BAKING SODA.

4. SMELLY HIKING BOOTS OR SHOES CAN ALSO BE FRESHENED. JUST SPRINKLE A LITTLE BAKING SODA IN THEM AND LEAVE OVERNIGHT.

5. TO REMOVE THE ODOR LEFT FROM CLEANING FISH, RUB A BIT OF DRY BAKING SODA ON YOUR HANDS, THEN WASH IN WARM, SOAPY WATER.

6. ONE POPULAR USE FOR BAKING SODA IS AS A FIRE EXTINGUISHER. IN CASE GREASE FROM THE CAMPFIRE OR CAMPSTOVE CATCHES FIRE, THROW HANDFULS OF DRY BAKING SODA ON THE FLAMES. NEVER USE WATER ON A GREASE, OIL OR GASOLINE FIRE.

© 1972 UNIVERSAL PRESS SYNDICATE

Mark Gregory

Natural Crafts

AN OLD-TIME CLAY THAT CHILDREN WILL HAVE A LOT OF FUN WITH CAN BE MADE WITH BAKING SODA.

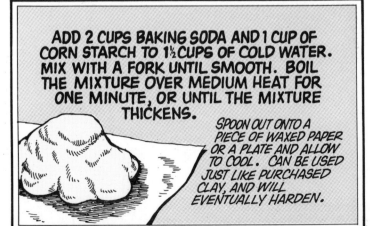

ADD 2 CUPS BAKING SODA AND 1 CUP OF CORN STARCH TO 1½ CUPS OF COLD WATER. MIX WITH A FORK UNTIL SMOOTH. BOIL THE MIXTURE OVER MEDIUM HEAT FOR ONE MINUTE, OR UNTIL THE MIXTURE THICKENS.

SPOON OUT ONTO A PIECE OF WAXED PAPER OR A PLATE AND ALLOW TO COOL. CAN BE USED JUST LIKE PURCHASED CLAY, AND WILL EVENTUALLY HARDEN.

6

SURVIVAL
AND SAFETY

TO THE EXPERIENCED WOODSMAN, HOME IS WHERE HE IS.

NATURAL FOODS

MANY PEOPLE HAVE GONE HUNGRY IN THE WOODS WITH ALL KINDS OF EDIBLE WILD PLANTS SURROUNDING THEM.

WILD ROSE

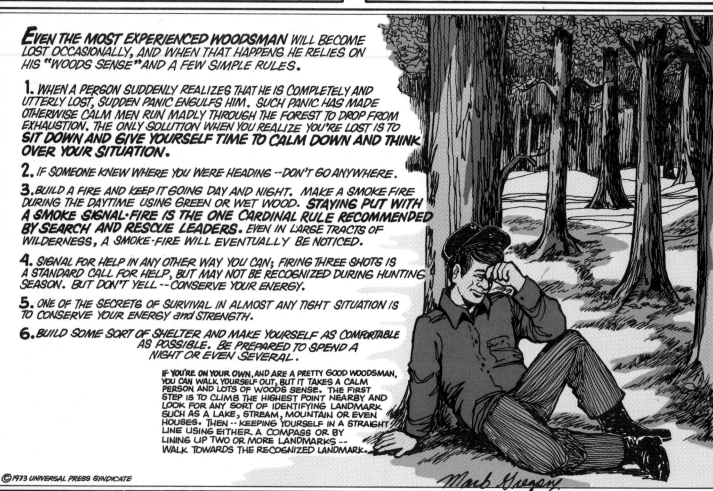

EVEN THE MOST EXPERIENCED WOODSMAN WILL BECOME LOST OCCASIONALLY, AND WHEN THAT HAPPENS HE RELIES ON HIS "WOODS SENSE" AND A FEW SIMPLE RULES.

1. WHEN A PERSON SUDDENLY REALIZES THAT HE IS COMPLETELY AND UTTERLY LOST, SUDDEN PANIC ENGULFS HIM. SUCH PANIC HAS MADE OTHERWISE CALM MEN RUN MADLY THROUGH THE FOREST TO DROP FROM EXHAUSTION. THE ONLY SOLUTION WHEN YOU REALIZE YOU'RE LOST IS TO **SIT DOWN AND GIVE YOURSELF TIME TO CALM DOWN AND THINK OVER YOUR SITUATION.**

2. IF SOMEONE KNEW WHERE YOU WERE HEADING -- DON'T GO ANYWHERE.

3. BUILD A FIRE AND KEEP IT GOING DAY AND NIGHT. MAKE A SMOKE-FIRE DURING THE DAYTIME USING GREEN OR WET WOOD. **STAYING PUT WITH A SMOKE SIGNAL-FIRE IS THE ONE CARDINAL RULE RECOMMENDED BY SEARCH AND RESCUE LEADERS.** EVEN IN LARGE TRACTS OF WILDERNESS, A SMOKE-FIRE WILL EVENTUALLY BE NOTICED.

4. SIGNAL FOR HELP IN ANY OTHER WAY YOU CAN; FIRING THREE SHOTS IS A STANDARD CALL FOR HELP, BUT MAY NOT BE RECOGNIZED DURING HUNTING SEASON. BUT DON'T YELL -- CONSERVE YOUR ENERGY.

5. ONE OF THE SECRETS OF SURVIVAL IN ALMOST ANY TIGHT SITUATION IS TO CONSERVE YOUR ENERGY and STRENGTH.

6. BUILD SOME SORT OF SHELTER AND MAKE YOURSELF AS COMFORTABLE AS POSSIBLE. BE PREPARED TO SPEND A NIGHT OR EVEN SEVERAL.

IF YOU'RE ON YOUR OWN, AND ARE A PRETTY GOOD WOODSMAN, YOU CAN WALK YOURSELF OUT, BUT IT TAKES A CALM PERSON AND LOTS OF WOODS SENSE. THE FIRST STEP IS TO CLIMB THE HIGHEST POINT NEARBY AND LOOK FOR ANY SORT OF IDENTIFYING LANDMARK SUCH AS A LAKE, STREAM, MOUNTAIN OR EVEN HOUSES. THEN -- KEEPING YOURSELF IN A STRAIGHT LINE USING EITHER A COMPASS OR BY LINING UP TWO OR MORE LANDMARKS -- WALK TOWARDS THE RECOGNIZED LANDMARK.

Mark Gregory

Natural Crafts

ONE EXCELLENT WAY OF SIGNALING IS TO BLOW ACROSS THE TOP OF A SPENT CARTRIDGE TO PRODUCE A PIERCING WHISTLE.

THE BEST METHOD OF SIGNALING HELP FROM AIR PATROLS IS TO FORM AN S·O·S ON THE GROUND USING ANY SORT OF MEANS FROM PILING ROCKS TO DIGGING A TRENCH IN THE SNOW.

LATE WINTER SUNLIGHT STIMULATES MILLIONS OF SNOW FLEAS WHICH FEED ON THE ALGAE GENERATED IN THE SNOW BY THE SUNLIGHT.

NATURAL FOODS

CARRY A BAG OF RAISINS OR DRIED FRUIT WHEN HEADING OUT INTO THE WINTER OUTDOORS. THEY'RE GREAT SNACKS AS WELL AS EXCELLENT EMERGENCY SURVIVAL FOOD.

WINTER OUTDOORS CAN BE A TIME OF GREAT FUN AND HEALTHFUL EXERCISE, BUT IT CAN ALSO BE EXTREMELY DANGEROUS. ONE OF THE WORSE DANGERS OF WINTER IS **DROWNING FROM FALLING THROUGH ICE.**

SKATERS OR ICE FISHERMEN SHOULD NEVER GET OUT ON A FROZEN LAKE WITHOUT EXAMINING THE ICE CAREFULLY FIRST. ON A LAKE IT TAKES AT LEAST 4 TO 5 INCHES OF CLEAR ICE TO SUPPORT AN ADULT'S WEIGHT.

YOUNGSTERS SHOULD NEVER SKATE OR PLAY ON A LAKE UNLESS IT HAS FIRST BEEN EXAMINED CAREFULLY BY ADULTS.

SHOULD YOU EVER FALL THROUGH A FROZEN·OVER LAKE OR OR STREAM, REMEMBER:

1. FIRST AND MOST IMPORTANT : **DON'T PANIC.**

2. WHEN YOU FEEL YOURSELF FALLING, SPREAD-EAGLE YOUR ARMS AND LEGS TO HELP PREVENT GOING COMPLETELY UNDER THE ICE.

3. AS SOON AS YOU SURFACE, OR AS QUICKLY AS YOU CAN, TRY TO GET YOUR ARMS OVER THE EDGE OF THE ICE. IF THE WEATHER IS EXTREMELY COLD, YOUR CLOTHING AND GLOVES MAY FREEZE TO THE ICE.

4. IF THE ICE IS TOO THIN TO SUPPORT YOUR WEIGHT, BREAK IT OFF UNTIL YOU REACH SOLID ICE.

5. KICK UP YOUR FEET IN A SWIMMING MOTION TO BRING YOUR BODY AS HORIZONTAL AS POSSIBLE, THEN TRY TO ROLL OUT AND AWAY ONTO SOLID ICE.

6. IF HELP IS NEARBY, GET THERE AS SOON AS POSSIBLE. IF YOUR CAR IS CLOSE, GET TO IT AND TURN ON THE HEATER.

7. IF YOU'RE BY YOURSELF AND TOO FAR FROM ANY HELP, START A FIRE IMMEDIATELY AND GATHER A GOOD SUPPLY OF FUEL AS SOON AS POSSIBLE. (NO ONE SHOULD BE OUTDOORS IN WINTER WITHOUT WATERPROOF MATCHES.)

IF YOU'RE TRAVELING AND MUST CROSS A FROZEN RIVER DO SO VERY CAUTIOUSLY. ICE TRAVEL ON RIVERS IS SELDOM SAFE, EVEN IN SUB-ZERO WEATHER BECAUSE THE RUNNING WATER ERODES THE ICE FROM BELOW, LEAVING DANGEROUSLY THIN POCKETS. IF YOU MUST CROSS A STREAM OR FROZEN LAKE YOU'RE NOT SURE ABOUT, CARRY A LONG THIN POLE AND CRAWL ACROSS THE ICE IN A SWIMMING MOTION. IF YOU'RE WITH A COMPANION, CROSS ABOUT 25 OR 30 FEET APART (SINGLE FILE) AND WITH A ROPE BETWEEN YOU.

IN THE EVENT YOU DO FALL THROUGH THE ICE -- AND IT WILL HAPPEN SOONER OR LATER TO ALMOST ANY OUTDOORSMAN WHO SPENDS MUCH TIME TRAVELING THE BACKWOODS IN WINTER -- KNOWING A FEW SIMPLE RULES MAY SAVE YOUR LIFE.

8. IF YOU CAN BUILD THE FIRE NEAR SOME SORT OF SHELTER, REMOVE YOUR CLOTHES AND WRING MOST OF THE WATER FROM THEM. IF NOT, LEAVE ON YOUR CLOTHES AND KEEP THE FIRE ROARING.

Mark Gregory

Natural Crafts

I ALWAYS CARRY A STURDY HUNTING KNIFE ANYTIME I'M TRAVELING OUTDOORS, SUMMER OR WINTER. IN AN EMERGENCY IT CAN BE JABBED INTO THE ICE AND WILL GIVE YOU LEVERAGE TO PULL YOURSELF OUT IN CASE OF A BREAKTHROUGH.

SOME OLD-TIMERS SUGGEST ROLLING IN FLUFFY SNOW IF YOU FALL THROUGH THE ICE. THE SNOW WILL STICK TO YOU AND FORM A TEMPORARY KIND OF INSULATION.

A BABY SNAKE GETS OUT OF ITS EGG BY MEANS OF A TEMPORARY EGG TOOTH, JUST AS A BABY CHICK DOES.

PECK PECK

SNAKES ARE A VALUABLE FRIEND TO MAN. A BLACKSNAKE IS A LIVING RAT TRAP AND IS COMMONLY CALLED A "RAT SNAKE."

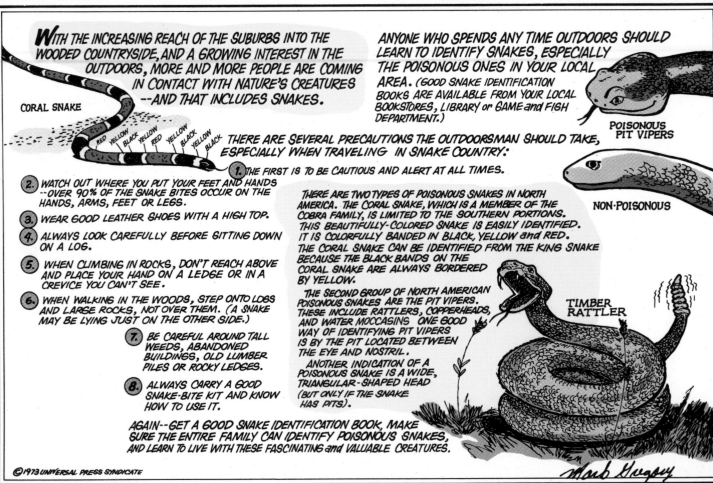

WITH THE INCREASING REACH OF THE SUBURBS INTO THE WOODED COUNTRYSIDE, AND A GROWING INTEREST IN THE OUTDOORS, MORE AND MORE PEOPLE ARE COMING IN CONTACT WITH NATURE'S CREATURES --AND THAT INCLUDES SNAKES.

CORAL SNAKE

RED YELLOW BLACK YELLOW RED YELLOW BLACK YELLOW BLACK

THERE ARE SEVERAL PRECAUTIONS THE OUTDOORSMAN SHOULD TAKE, ESPECIALLY WHEN TRAVELING IN SNAKE COUNTRY:

1. THE FIRST IS TO BE CAUTIOUS AND ALERT AT ALL TIMES.

2. WATCH OUT WHERE YOU PUT YOUR FEET AND HANDS --OVER 90% OF THE SNAKE BITES OCCUR ON THE HANDS, ARMS, FEET OR LEGS.

3. WEAR GOOD LEATHER SHOES WITH A HIGH TOP.

4. ALWAYS LOOK CAREFULLY BEFORE SITTING DOWN ON A LOG.

5. WHEN CLIMBING IN ROCKS, DON'T REACH ABOVE AND PLACE YOUR HAND ON A LEDGE OR IN A CREVICE YOU CAN'T SEE.

6. WHEN WALKING IN THE WOODS, STEP ONTO LOGS AND LARGE ROCKS, NOT OVER THEM. (A SNAKE MAY BE LYING JUST ON THE OTHER SIDE.)

7. BE CAREFUL AROUND TALL WEEDS, ABANDONED BUILDINGS, OLD LUMBER PILES OR ROCKY LEDGES.

8. ALWAYS CARRY A GOOD SNAKE-BITE KIT AND KNOW HOW TO USE IT.

ANYONE WHO SPENDS ANY TIME OUTDOORS SHOULD LEARN TO IDENTIFY SNAKES, ESPECIALLY THE POISONOUS ONES IN YOUR LOCAL AREA. (GOOD SNAKE IDENTIFICATION BOOKS ARE AVAILABLE FROM YOUR LOCAL BOOKSTORES, LIBRARY or GAME and FISH DEPARTMENT.)

POISONOUS PIT VIPERS

NON-POISONOUS

THERE ARE TWO TYPES OF POISONOUS SNAKES IN NORTH AMERICA. THE CORAL SNAKE, WHICH IS A MEMBER OF THE COBRA FAMILY, IS LIMITED TO THE SOUTHERN PORTIONS. THIS BEAUTIFULLY-COLORED SNAKE IS EASILY IDENTIFIED. IT IS COLORFULLY BANDED IN BLACK, YELLOW and RED. THE CORAL SNAKE CAN BE IDENTIFIED FROM THE KING SNAKE BECAUSE THE BLACK BANDS ON THE CORAL SNAKE ARE ALWAYS BORDERED BY YELLOW.

THE SECOND GROUP OF NORTH AMERICAN POISONOUS SNAKES ARE THE PIT VIPERS. THESE INCLUDE RATTLERS, COPPERHEADS, AND WATER MOCCASINS. ONE GOOD WAY OF IDENTIFYING PIT VIPERS IS BY THE PIT LOCATED BETWEEN THE EYE AND NOSTRIL.

ANOTHER INDICATION OF A POISONOUS SNAKE IS A WIDE, TRIANGULAR-SHAPED HEAD (BUT ONLY IF THE SNAKE HAS PITS).

TIMBER RATTLER

AGAIN--GET A GOOD SNAKE IDENTIFICATION BOOK, MAKE SURE THE ENTIRE FAMILY CAN IDENTIFY POISONOUS SNAKES, AND LEARN TO LIVE WITH THESE FASCINATING and VALUABLE CREATURES.

© 1973 UNIVERSAL PRESS SYNDICATE

Mark Gregory

SNAKES ARE NOT "SLIMY," THEIR SKINS ARE DRY AND VERY CLEAN.

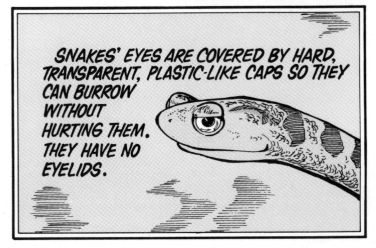

SNAKES' EYES ARE COVERED BY HARD, TRANSPARENT, PLASTIC-LIKE CAPS SO THEY CAN BURROW WITHOUT HURTING THEM. THEY HAVE NO EYELIDS.

THE BABIES OF MANY PIT VIPERS SUCH AS RATTLESNAKES OR COPPERHEADS CAN STRIKE AT BIRTH, AND CARRY POISON.

SINCE SNAKES GROW STEADILY, THEY MUST CHANGE THEIR SKIN, WHICH DOES NOT GROW, AT AN INTERVAL OF SIX WEEKS (EXCEPT DURING HIBERNATION). THE NEW SKIN FORMS UNDER THE OLD.

POISONOUS SNAKES ARE PROBABLY THE MOST FEARED OF WILD CREATURES. BUT THE INCIDENT OF SNAKE BITE WITH A RESULTING DEATH IS LOW IN NORTH AMERICA. THERE ARE AROUND 2400 SNAKE BITE CASES PER YEAR AND OF THESE LESS THAN ONE PER CENT PROVE FATAL. MOST OF THE SNAKE-BITE CASES THAT PROVE FATAL ARE CAUSED BY NON-TREATMENT OR THE VICTIM'S POOR HEALTH. A CHILD WHOSE BODY ISN'T LARGE ENOUGH TO ABSORB THE TOXIN CAN BECOME A FATALITY.

ANYONE WHO SPENDS MUCH TIME IN THE OUTDOORS SHOULD KNOW HOW TO IDENTIFY POISONOUS SNAKES, HOW TO STAY AWAY FROM THEM AND SHOULD ALWAYS CARRY A SNAKE-BITE KIT and KNOW HOW TO USE IT.

1. THE FIRST STEP IN CASE OF SNAKE BITE IS TO TRY AND CALM THE VICTIM OR YOURSELF. SNAKE BITES USUALLY BRING ON PURE TERROR and THE SHOCK CAN BE WORSE THAN THE BITE.

2. IF POSSIBLE, KILL THE SNAKE AND IDENTIFY WHETHER POISONOUS OR NOT.

3. EXAMINE THE BITE WOUND. AS SHOWN, POISONOUS SNAKES HAVE NO OUTER UPPER TEETH, ONLY FANGS. NON-POISONOUS SNAKES HAVE TWO ROWS OF TEETH.

4. FIRST AID TREATMENT MUST BEGIN AT ONCE.

5. IF POSSIBLE, APPLY A TOURNIQUET BETWEEN THE BITE AND THE HEART. THE TOURNIQUET SHOULD BE OF SOME WIDE MATERIAL and SHOULD BE LEFT LOOSE ENOUGH SO THAT A FINGER CAN BE SLIPPED UNDER IT. LOOSEN THE TOURNIQUET AT LEAST TWO OUT OF EVERY TEN MINUTES. AND DON'T KEEP IT ON LONGER THAN ONE HOUR.

Snake Bite Wounds

POISONOUS   NON-POISONOUS

© 1973 UNIVERSAL PRESS SYNDICATE

6. MAKE A SMALL INCISION AT EACH FANG MARK, AND ONLY AS DEEP AS THE PENETRATION OF THE FANGS. THERE IS NO NEED TO MAKE A LARGE X. THE CUT MUST BE MADE IMMEDIATELY AFTER THE BITE OR IS INEFFECTIVE. THE CUTS MADE BY THE RAZOR WILL HARDLY BE FELT DUE TO THE EFFECT OF THE BITE. KEEP THE CUTS AS SMALL AS POSSIBLE.

7. BEGIN SUCTION IMMEDIATELY, USING EITHER A SUCTION CUP FROM A SNAKE BITE KIT OR YOUR MOUTH. APPLY SUCTION FOR AT LEAST ONE HOUR.

8. PLACE THE BITE UNDER AN ICE BATH FOR THE SECOND HOUR AFTER THE BITE, THEN STOP AT THE END OF THE SECOND HOUR (NO LONGER). ICE PACKS MAY BE USED TO KEEP THE BITE COOL FOR 24 TO 48 HOURS.

9. IF AT ALL POSSIBLE, GET TO A HOSPITAL AND GET A SHOT OF ANTIVENIN.

CAUTION: THERE IS PROBABLY MORE HARM CAUSED BY IMPROPERLY APPLIED TOURNIQUETS, GERM-LADEN RAZOR BLADES and UNTESTED ANTIVENIN THAN SNAKEBITES --- SO PLEASE KNOW WHAT YOU'RE DOING.

Mark Gregory

Natural Crafts

ALWAYS CARRY A GOOD FIRST AID KIT AND SNAKE-BITE KIT WHEN HEADING INTO SNAKE COUNTRY.

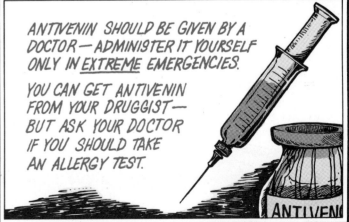

ANTIVENIN SHOULD BE GIVEN BY A DOCTOR — ADMINISTER IT YOURSELF ONLY IN <u>EXTREME</u> EMERGENCIES.

YOU CAN GET ANTIVENIN FROM YOUR DRUGGIST — BUT ASK YOUR DOCTOR IF YOU SHOULD TAKE AN ALLERGY TEST.

ANTIVENIN

WITH HIS WIDE, "SPLAYED" FEET THE MOOSE CAN OFTEN TRAVEL ACROSS DANGEROUS QUAGMIRES.

IF YOU'RE TRAVELING IN QUICKSAND OR QUAGMIRE COUNTRY, CARRY A LONG POLE AND PROBE THE GROUND AHEAD OF YOU.

QUICKSAND IS ONE OF THE MOST WIDELY PUBLICIZED OUTDOOR DANGERS, BUT ONE OF THE LEAST UNDERSTOOD.

QUICKSAND IS ACTUALLY FINE SAND FLOATING "ON TOP OF AND IN WATER." THE WATER IS USUALLY FROM A WEAK UNDERGROUND SPRING AND IS MOVING UP WITH ENOUGH PRESSURE TO KEEP THE GRAINS OF SAND SUSPENDED AND MOVING OR "QUICK." A QUAGMIRE IS SIMILAR TO QUICKSAND. IT IS COMPOSED OF DECAYED MATERIAL OR MUD SUSPENDED BY UNDERGROUND WATER.

THE FIRST RULE IN EITHER CASE IS TO REMEMBER YOU'RE BASICALLY IN WATER AND YOU CAN "SWIM" OR CRAWL FREE.

THE MOST IMPORTANT RULE IS TO NOT PANIC. USUALLY WHEN YOU FIND YOURSELF IN QUICKSAND, YOU'VE ALREADY SUNK UP TO YOUR WAIST AND STRUGGLING WILL ONLY CAUSE YOU TO SINK FASTER.

IMMEDIATELY THROW YOURSELF OUT BACKWARDS FLAT ON THE SAND, ARMS AND LEGS SPREAD AS WIDE AS POSSIBLE.

WHILE YOU FLOAT ON THE SAND TRY TO GENTLY EXTRICATE EACH LEG, THEN ROLL AND TRY TO SWIM OUT.

THE MAIN THING IS TO PREVENT TIRING YOURSELF, SO TAKE YOUR TIME AND REST OFTEN.

PANIC-STRICKEN STRUGGLING ONLY CAUSES YOU TO SINK "BY GRAVITY" DEEPER INTO THE MIRE. IN TRYING TO PULL OUT ONE LEG YOU WILL ONLY FORCE THE OTHER LEG (WITH ALL YOUR WEIGHT) DOWN FURTHER.

AVOID SUDDEN MOTIONS--TAKE YOUR TIME.

USUALLY QUICKSAND OR QUAGMIRE BEDS ARE NOT TOO LARGE, SO DON'T GIVE UP.

QUICKSAND OR QUAGMIRE ARE FOUND ALL OVER THE NORTH AMERICAN CONTINENT, SO LEARN TO WATCH FOR THEM. QUICKSAND IS MOST OFTEN FOUND AROUND AREAS WHERE WATER RISES TO THE SURFACE OF THE EARTH, FOR INSTANCE IN STREAM BEDS, WELLS and AROUND SPRINGS. BE ESPECIALLY CAREFUL IN SANDY SOIL AROUND THESE CONDITIONS.

QUAGMIRES ARE OFTEN FOUND AROUND OLD WATERHOLES, IN MUSKEG COUNTRY AND AROUND SWAMPS, MARSHES and TIDAL FLATS.

Mark Gregory

PITS OF QUICKSAND OR QUAGMIRES ARE NATURAL DEATH PITS FOR ANIMALS BECAUSE THEY CAN'T THINK AND IN THEIR STRUGGLE ONLY DIG THEMSELVES DEEPER INTO THE MIRE.

MANY BONES OF PREHISTORIC ANIMALS FOUND TODAY ARE FROM OLD QUICKSAND BOGS.

7

DECORATIVE
AND USEFUL CRAFTS

ROADSIDES and HIGHWAY RIGHT OF WAYS PROVIDE MUCH NEEDED WILDLIFE HABITAT. LET THEM GROW DURING THE NESTING SEASONS.

NATURAL FOODS

CATTAIL ROOTS ARE BOTH DELICIOUS AND NUTRITIOUS. CENTER LUMP CAN BE COOKED AND EATEN LIKE A POTATO. LONG ROOTS CAN BE CUT AND GROUND INTO "CATTAIL FLOUR."

This Thanksgiving Decorate Your Home

with NATURAL MATERIALS gathered from the country roadsides, marshes and fields.

© 1971 Universal Press Syndicate

Milkweed

MILKWEED IS ANOTHER EASILY FOUND PLANT. IT CAN BE USED WHOLE OR THE PODS MAY BE REMOVED AND USED ALONE AS DECORATIONS.

DRIED INDIAN CORN
is, of course, traditional.

BUFFALO GRASSES OR MARSH GRASSES
may also be used decoratively.

Cattails

THE MOST COMMONLY USED PLANT IS THE CATTAIL. CUT OFF JUST AT GROUND LEVEL TO KEEP LEAVES ATTACHED.

Bittersweet

SPRIGS OF BITTERSWEET ADD A TRADITIONAL SPOT OF COLOR. (DO NOT USE AROUND CHILDREN AS THE SEEDS ARE POISONOUS.)

Natural Crafts

CATTAIL LEAVES ARE THE TRADITIONAL MATERIAL FOR RUSH-BOTTOM CHAIRS.

1. THE LEAVES MUST BE GATHERED WHILE GREEN.

2. BUNDLES OF LEAVES ARE HUNG UPSIDE DOWN IN A COOL, DRY SPOT TO DRY. THEN, BEFORE USING, THEY ARE SOAKED IN WATER.

3. STRANDS ARE TWISTED TOGETHER AND WOVEN TO MAKE THE SEAT.

BUY A *"BALLED"* CHRISTMAS TREE; IT NOT ONLY WILL KEEP GREENER INSIDE THE HOUSE, BUT YOU CAN *PLANT IT WHEN CHRISTMAS IS OVER!*

MAKE Old Fashioned Popcorn Balls LIKE GRANDMOTHER DID. BOIL A CUP OF LIGHT SYRUP AND ⅓ CUP OF HONEY. POUR OVER POPCORN AND FORM INTO BALLS.

Have A Natural Christmas

DECORATE YOUR TREE AND HOME WITH NATURAL DECORATIONS JUST LIKE GRANDMA DID YEARS AGO. THE KIDS WILL LOVE IT! YOU CAN ALSO MAKE UNUSUAL WRAPPING PAPER AND CARDS WITH NATURAL MATERIALS AND OLD-TIME METHODS.

Traditional Decorations Include: POPCORN ON A STRING (for variety alternate with cranberries)

A FAVORITE WITH ALL KIDS IS A TREE FULL OF **GINGERBREAD MEN.**

UNUSUAL DECORATIONS ARE SYCAMORE BALLS DIPPED IN BRIGHT POSTER PAINT, THEN IN FLAKES OF GLITTER.

©1971 Universal Press Syndicate

Wrapping Paper

A CHILD'S HAND OR FOOT DIPPED IN POSTER PAINT AND PLACED ON PAPER WILL MAKE A WRAPPING PAPER ANY GRANDPARENT WILL CHERISH.

A MANTLEPIECE DECORATION CAN BE A BARE BRANCH DIPPED IN THIN STARCH AND SPRINKLED WITH FLAKES OF MICA OR GLITTER.

Cards

1. PAINT ONE SIDE OF A TWIG OF PINE NEEDLES WITH GREEN POSTER PAINT.

2. LAY ON A WHITE FOLDED CARD AND PRESS WITH A BOARD.

3. PRINT YOUR MESSAGE INSIDE.

Natural Crafts

MAKE PINECONE FIREPLACE GIFTS THAT BURN WITH BRIGHT BLUE and GREEN FLAMES

1. Mix small amounts of COPPER SULPHATE (Blue) or BORAX (Green) with shellac.

2. Paint or dip cones in mixture and hang to dry.

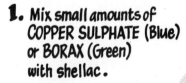

3. Tie several of each kind together with bright ribbons.

MANY WILDFLOWERS AND "WEED FLOWERS" ARE GREAT WHEN THEY ARE DRIED AND ARRANGED IN "NATURAL ARRANGEMENTS."

DRYING FLOWERS IS AN ANCIENT CRAFT DATING BACK TO THE TIMES WHEN MANY PLANTS WERE DRIED AND USED FOR MEDICINAL PURPOSES.

DRIED FLOWERS ARE AN EASY WAY OF PRESERVING A TOUCH OF SUMMER COLOR FOR WINTER, AND DRYING FLOWERS IS AN EASY AND FUN ACTIVITY.

MANY KINDS OF FLOWERS CAN BE DRIED, BUT STRAWFLOWERS ARE THE EASIEST, LAST THE LONGEST, AND PROVIDE THE MOST COLOR.

THERE ARE SEVERAL WAYS OF DRYING FLOWERS, BUT AIR DRYING IS THE SIMPLEST AND OLDEST METHOD.

1. GATHER FLOWERS WHEN THEY ARE ABOUT HALF OPEN, AND ON A HOT, DRY DAY. ALL LEAVES SHOULD BE STRIPPED FROM THE PLANT.

2. TIE BUNCHES OF FLOWERS TIGHTLY TOGETHER WITH STRING.

3. STRING A CLOTHESLINE ACROSS A HOT, DRY ROOM SUCH AS AN ATTIC (OR CLOSET -- IF IT IS WARM AND DRY) AND SUSPEND THE BUNCHES OF FLOWERS UPSIDE DOWN, TYING THEM SECURELY TO THE CLOTHESLINE.

4. SPACE THE TIED BUNCHES OF FLOWERS FAR ENOUGH APART TO ALLOW FOR GOOD AIR CIRCULATION.

5. ALLOW THE FLOWERS TO DRY FOR THREE OR FOUR WEEKS. IF THE PLANTS ARE COARSE AND WEEDY, THEY MAY TAKE A BIT LONGER.

6. THE PIECES OF STEM LEFT ON THE FLOWERS ARE REINFORCED BY TYING FLORIST WIRE TO THEM, WRAPPING THEM WITH GREEN FLORIST TAPE.

7. THE STEMS OF SMALL FLOWERS CAN BE WRAPPED TOGETHER TO PRODUCE A COMPACT ATTRACTIVE ARRANGE-MENT THAT CAN BE PLACED IN A SMALL CONTAINER.

8. PLACE THE DRIED FLOWERS IN AN ATTRACTIVE VASE OR OTHER CON-TAINER, AND YOU'VE GOT A BEAUTIFUL DECORATION -- AND IT'S EASY AND ECONOMICAL.

9. ALL DRIED FLOWERS WILL FADE IN TIME -- BUT THEY WILL LAST LONGER IF THEY'RE NOT PLACED NEAR DIRECT SUNLIGHT OR NEAR HEAT REGISTERS.

10. TO GIVE ADDED PROTECTION, SPRAY SEVERAL COATS OF HAIR SPRAY ONTO THE ARRANGEMENT.

Mark Gregory

Natural Crafts

PRESSING FLOWERS IS ANOTHER WAY OF PRESERVING THEIR BEAUTY AND COLOR. THE RESULTS CAN BE USED IN ANY NUMBER OF WAYS, FROM PRESSED FLOWER PICTURES TO DECORATIONS FOR WASTEBASKETS, ETC.

1. GATHER FLOWERS AS NEEDED AND PLACE THEM BETWEEN SHEETS OF WHITE CARDBOARD. PLACE THESE "MATS" UNDER A HEAVY WEIGHT SUCH AS A STACK OF BOOKS.

2. AFTER SEVERAL WEEKS, REMOVE AND ARRANGE AS DESIRED.

THIS WAS A FAVORITE WITH YOUR GRANDMOTHER.

THERE IS A CLOSENESS WITH THE EARTH WHEN YOU MAKE POTTERY FROM CLAY YOU'VE DUG WITH YOUR OWN HANDS.

NATURAL ICE CREAM

- 3 EGGS
- 3 CUPS CREAM
- ¾ CUP HONEY
- 1½ TSP. VANILLA

BEAT EGG YOLKS, ADD HONEY. BLEND IN CREAM and VANILLA FLAVORING. FREEZE UNTIL FIRM. PLACE IN A CHILLED BOWL, ADD BEATEN EGG WHITES. BEAT UNTIL SMOOTH, POUR IN FREEZER TRAY. FREEZE UNTIL FIRM.

WORKING WITH CLAY IS ONE OF MAN'S OLDEST CRAFTS AND ONE THAT ANYONE ANY AGE CAN ENJOY. CLAY CAN BE USED PURELY AS A RECREATION FORM BY YOUNGSTERS OR BY ANYONE TO CREATE BEAUTIFUL, DECORATIVE and PRACTICAL OBJECTS FOR THE HOME. INSTEAD OF BUYING A BATCH OF CLAY, TRY GATHERING YOURS NATURALLY. IT'S EASY AND FUN, AND YOU'LL BE PRACTICING SOMETHING EARLIER CIVILIZATIONS ACCEPTED AS A WAY OF LIFE.

VARIOUS FORMS OF CLAY ARE FOUND ALL OVER THE WORLD AND CAN BE ANY COLOR FROM WHITE TO RED, TAN or EVEN GRAY DEPENDING ON THE MINERALS IT CONTAINS.

GOOD SPOTS TO LOOK FOR CLAY DEPOSITS ARE IN THE UNDERCUT BANKS OF STREAM BEDS, AROUND CONSTRUCTION AND ROAD BUILDING SITES, OR ANY PLACE WHERE THE TOPSOIL HAS BEEN CUT AWAY TO REVEAL THE LOWER "STRATUM."

TO TEST HOW GOOD A DEPOSIT OF CLAY IS, DIG OUT A HANDFUL AND SQUEEZE AND TWIST IT. IF IT IS PLASTIC AND WORKABLE YOU'VE GOT A GOOD DEPOSIT OF WORKABLE CLAY. IF IT CRUMBLES, ADD A BIT MORE WATER AND TRY AGAIN.

1. WHEN YOU'VE FOUND A CLAY DEPOSIT, DIG OUT THE AMOUNT YOU NEED AND SPREAD IT OUT IN A THIN LAYER TO DRY.

2. WHEN DRY BREAK IT INTO TINY PIECES AND ADD TO WATER UNTIL MIXTURE IS "SOUPY."

3. POUR THIS "SLIP" THROUGH A COARSE WIRE SCREEN SEVERAL TIMES TO REMOVE ROCKS, LEAVES, ETC.

4. POUR THE THIN CLAY OUT ONTO A CLEAN CONCRETE SLAB AND ALLOW SOME OF THE MOISTURE TO EVAPORATE.

5. PICK UP THE CLAY AND WORK IT, SLAMMING IT DOWN ON THE SLAB AND TEARING IT APART, WORKING IT WITH YOUR HANDS TO REMOVE ALL BUBBLES AND TO EVEN IT OUT.

THE CLAY THEN CAN BE KEPT IN A TIED PLASTIC BAG AND USED AS NEEDED. IT CAN BE MOLDED, SHAPED INTO BOWLS, MUGS, PLATES, STATUES OR ANY OTHER ITEM YOU DESIRE.

Mark Gregory

Natural Crafts

TO MAKE UTENSILS THAT WILL HOLD WATER YOU MUST FIRE THEM, OR EXPOSE THEM TO EXTREME HEAT.

ONE GOOD WAY OF FIRING IS TO MAKE AN OUTDOOR KILN SUCH AS THE INDIANS DID. MERELY BUILD A LARGE OPEN FIRE AND COVER THE POTS WITH HEAPS OF HOT COALS.

(OR YOU MAY HAVE CERAMIC SHOPS FIRE YOUR CLAY ITEMS FOR YOU.)

To Scent Homemade Soap, POUR IN A FEW DROPS OF YOUR FAVORITE PERFUME (ANY THAT DOES NOT CONTAIN ALCOHOL), OR STORE THE SOAP WITH A FEW LEAVES OR PETALS OF YOUR FAVORITE FRAGRANT FLOWER OR HERB.

NATURAL FOODS

HOMEMADE PEANUT BUTTER is the best.

USE A SEED GRINDER OR ELECTRIC BLENDER TO GRIND NUTS. USE UNROASTED NUTS (BUT NOT GREEN NUTS). ADD SOY OIL (available from natural food stores) OR ANY GOOD VEGETABLE OIL AND BLEND TO TASTE. FOR UNUSUAL TASTE, ADD OTHER NUTS OR SEEDS SUCH AS WALNUTS, PECANS, SUNFLOWER SEEDS, ETC.

WITH A LITTLE PRACTICE YOU CAN MAKE YOUR OWN PURE HOMEMADE SOAP THAT IS BETTER THAN ANY YOU CAN BUY, AND YOU CAN USE FAT FROM MEAT TRIMMINGS OR EVEN COOKING GREASE YOU ORDINARILY WOULD DISCARD. YOU CAN USE LARD (PORK FAT), TALLOW (BEEF FAT), OR A MIXTURE.

SOAP

Step 1. SAVE ALL TRIMMINGS FROM MEATS, AS WELL AS COOKING GREASE. KEEP REFRIGERATED. TO CLEAN COOKING GREASE — HEAT, ALLOW IMPURITIES TO SETTLE, POUR CLEAN GREASE OFF THE TOP. ANY FATS OR GREASE USED IN SOAP MAKING MUST BE FREE OF DIRT, LEAN MEAT, AND MUST NOT BE "SPOILED."

RECIPE for 9 POUNDS of SOAP

- 2½ PINTS of COLD WATER
- 1 CAN of LYE (IN FLAKE FORM) [13 OZ. CAN]
- 6 LBS. of TALLOW or LARD

Step 2. DISSOLVE THE CAN OF LYE IN THE WATER IN A PYREX MIXING BOWL. STIR SLOWLY AND *BE CAREFUL — THE LYE IS CAUSTIC AND CAN CAUSE BURNS!* WASH WITH PLENTY OF COLD WATER IF YOU SHOULD SPLASH LYE ON YOURSELF.

Step 3. SET LYE-WATER ASIDE AND MELT GREASE OR FATS TO A CLEAR LIQUID. POUR CLEAR LIQUID THROUGH A KITCHEN STRAINER, ALLOW TO COOL UNTIL THE LIQUID BEGINS TO OFFER RESISTANCE TO STIRRING.

Temperature Chart:

FAT	FAT TEMP.	LYE TEMP.
Lard or Soft Fat	98-100°F.	77-80°F.
Half Lard, Half Tallow	105-110°F.	83-86°F.
Tallow	125-130°F.	93-96°F.

Step 4. WHEN BOTH LYE MIXTURE AND GREASE REACH TEMPERATURE ON CHART (ACCORDING TO TYPE OF TALLOW OR LARD), VERY CAREFULLY POUR THE LYE MIXTURE INTO THE MELTED GREASE IN A STEADY THIN STREAM, STIRRING CONSTANTLY. CONTINUE STIRRING UNTIL MIXTURE REACHES CONSISTENCY OF THICK HONEY. (10 to 15 MINUTES)

Step 5. POUR THE THICKENED SOAP INTO THE WOOD FRAME LINED WITH A WET COTTON SHEET. COVER THE FRAME WITH A CLEAN BOARD, THEN WITH NEWSPAPERS, AN OLD BLANKET, AND ALLOW THE SOAP TO COOL GRADUALLY. IN TWO WEEKS REMOVE SOAP FROM MOLD AND CUT INTO CAKES.

Mark Gregory

© 1972 Universal Press Syndicate

DON'T THROW AWAY THOSE WOOD ASHES FROM YOUR FIREPLACE. USE THEM TO MAKE A LYE SOLUTION FOR SOAP MAKING.

ASH

STEP 1. YOU WILL NEED A FIVE GALLON CAN WITH A FEW DRAIN HOLES PUNCHED IN THE CENTER OF THE BOTTOM.

STEP 2. PLACE A 5 INCH LAYER OF STRAW IN THE CAN, THEN FILL THE CAN WITH ASHES. PLACE CAN ON TOP OF ANOTHER 5 GALLON CAN AND POUR WATER ON THE ASHES. EACH DAY POUR ON MORE WATER AS IT IS ABSORBED. WHEN THE BOTTOM CAN IS FULL OF "LYE WATER," REMOVE THE SOLUTION AND BOIL IT UNTIL A PIECE OF RAW POTATO WILL FLOAT IN IT.

Bayberry Scent

1. CRUSH BERRIES AND BOIL FOR 10 OR 15 MINUTES.

2. STRAIN THROUGH CLOTH AND ALLOW TO COOL. *REMOVE WAX FROM TOP.*

NATURAL FOODS

RAW HONEY IS A PURE SWEETENER AND A SUBSTITUTE FOR SUGAR. USE ONLY ½ AS MUCH HONEY AS YOU WOULD SUGAR IN YOUR FAVORITE RECIPES.

CLOVER HONEY IS THE SWEETEST HONEY.

Make Hand-Dipped Candles

THE SAME WAY YOUR GREAT-GRANDMOTHER DID. IT'S EASY!

IMPORTANT—ALWAYS TAKE THE UTMOST CARE IN HANDLING CANDLES.

1. MAKE A DIPPING FRAME FROM A COAT HANGER – TIE SOFT COTTON TWINE TO FRAME.

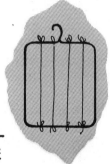

2. WAX MUST BE MELTED IN A DOUBLE-BOILER ARRANGEMENT. *USE A DISCARDED ANTI-FREEZE CAN SUSPENDED IN A HOME-CANNER...*

Never melt wax over an OPEN FLAME!

3. BREAK PARAFFIN OR PURCHASED WAX INTO CAN. ADD CRAYONS FOR COLORING. FILL CANNER WITH WATER, HEAT WAX TO 175° F. USE A CANDY THERMOMETER TO CHECK TEMPERATURE.

4. DIP THE DIPPING FRAME DOWN INTO THE WAX, THEN HANG IN A COOL SPOT FOR 5 MINUTES.

5. AFTER THE FIRST 10 DIPS EVERY OTHER DIP SHOULD BE A HALF DIP. 30 DIPS PRODUCES A CANDLE.

6. CLIP CANDLES FROM BOTTOM OF FRAME AND ALLOW TO HANG FOR A COUPLE OF DAYS.

Natural Crafts

MAKE A CANDLE HOLDER FROM THE TOP OF A FRUIT JUICE CAN.

1. REMOVE CAN TOP and DRAW PATTERN ON IT WITH CRAYON...

2. CUT PETALS WITH TIN SNIPS AND FILE THE EDGES SMOOTH.

3. CURVE PETALS AROUND PIPE OR CHAIR RUNG.

4. PAINT FLAT BLACK, PUSH CANDLE INTO PLACE.

THE WILD ANIMALS WERE CONSIDERED "BROTHERS" BY INDIAN HUNTERS BECAUSE THEY DEPENDED ON THEM FOR SURVIVAL.

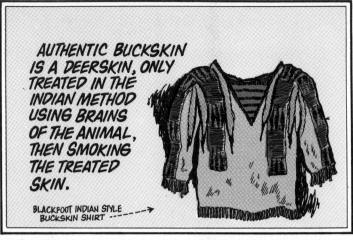

AUTHENTIC BUCKSKIN IS A DEERSKIN, ONLY TREATED IN THE INDIAN METHOD USING BRAINS OF THE ANIMAL, THEN SMOKING THE TREATED SKIN.

BLACKFOOT INDIAN STYLE BUCKSKIN SHIRT --->

TANNING ANIMAL HIDES FOR MAKING LEATHER MOCCASINS, SHIRTS, COATS, AND HUNDREDS OF OTHER ITEMS WAS ONE OF THE MOST VALUABLE SKILLS THE EARLY PIONEERS AND INDIANS KNEW, AND MANY OF THE OLD PROCESSES HAVE REMAINED UNCHANGED TO THIS DAY.

THIS IS ONE OF THE METHODS USED --AND MAY BE USED TODAY -- TO PRODUCE A "BUCKSKIN" TYPE OF LEATHER FROM A DEER OR ELK HIDE, OR A CALF-SKIN SECURED FROM YOUR LOCAL BUTCHER OR SLAUGHTER HOUSE.

1. SPREAD THE SKIN OUT, FLESH SIDE UP.

2. REMOVE ALL DIRT, FLESH, FAT, ETC., USING A DULL KNIFE TO SCRAPE.

3. COVER WITH SALT (AT LEAST ONE POUND TO EACH POUND OF HIDE).

4. FOLD HIDE TOGETHER (FLESH-TO-FLESH), AND THEN ROLL UP AND PLACE SO IT WILL DRAIN.

5. AFTER ONE DAY UNROLL, RESALT, SPREAD OUT IN A FLAT, DRY, COOL, AIRY PLACE AND ALLOW TO DRY. IT WILL KEEP UNTIL YOU ARE READY TO TAN. (IF YOU WISH TO TAN A FRESH SKIN, SOAK OVERNIGHT IN SALT WATER RATHER THAN SALTING AND ALLOWING TO DRY.)

6. COVER THE HAIR WITH A 2-INCH THICK LAYER OF WOOD ASHES. DAMPEN WITH SOFT WATER (RAIN WATER OR CREEK WATER). ROLL THE HIDE UP, HAIR INSIDE, TIE TIGHTLY AND LEAVE IN A DAMP SPOT FOR 3 OR 4 DAYS.

©1972 UNIVERSAL PRESS SYNDICATE

UNROLL AND SCRAPE OFF THE LOOSENED HAIR.

CAUTION: FOR THIS AND ALL TANNING STEPS, USE RUBBER GLOVES! THEY WILL NOT ONLY PROTECT YOU FROM THE VARIOUS MATERIALS, BUT FROM CATCHING A POSSIBLE DISEASE CARRIED BY THE ANIMAL.

7. SOAK THE CLEANED AND DE-HAIRED SKIN OVERNIGHT IN COLD SALT WATER.

8. PLACE IN A TANNING SOLUTION MADE UP OF A COUPLE OF CAKES OF NAPTHA SOAP AND A COUPLE OF PINTS OF NEATSFOOT OIL DISSOLVED IN ABOUT 4 GALLONS OF WARM WATER. LEAVE HIDES IN SOLUTION FOR 3 TO 4 DAYS, STIRRING OCCASIONALLY TO MAKE SURE ALL OF THE HIDE IS COVERED.

9. REMOVE THE HIDE, SQUEEZE DRY, THEN SCRAPE WITH A DULL KNIFE. WORK IT BACK AND FORTH OVER A CLEAN, DEBARKED LOG OR THE ROUNDED END OF A STAKE SET IN THE GROUND TO SOFTEN IT.

10. RETURN THE HIDE TO THE TANNING SOLUTION FOR 3 MORE DAYS, THEN REMOVE AND AGAIN SOFTEN ON STAKE AND WITH KNIFE.

11. SMOKE THE SKIN LAID OVER A TENT-LIKE FRAMEWORK OF GREEN BRANCHES. USE A SMALL FIRE AND KEEP IT COVERED WITH GREEN SHAVINGS OR BRANCHES TO PRODUCE A LOT OF SMOKE. SMOKING THE SKIN FOR THREE TO FOUR HOURS WILL GIVE THE SKIN A BETTER COLOR AND ODOR.

Mark Gregory

Natural Crafts

BUCKSKIN - Indian Method

1. CLEAN SKIN AND REMOVE HAIR BY SOAKING IN DAMPENED WOOD ASHES.

2. BOIL THE BRAINS OF ANIMAL AND MASH IN SOFT WATER TO MAKE TANNING SOLUTION.

3. SOAK HIDE IN TANNING LIQUID, WORKING IT FOR A COUPLE OF HOURS TO INSURE LIQUID PENETRATES ALL OF THE HIDE. THEN ALLOW TO SOAK OVERNIGHT AND WORK AGAIN.

4. STRETCH SKIN TO DRY IT, THEN ROLL AND ALLOW TO SET FOR A COUPLE OF WEEKS.

5. UNROLL AND SMOKE SKIN ON BOTH SIDES.

6. RINSE IN SOFT CREEK OR RAIN WATER, THEN STRETCH UNTIL DRY, AND WORK OVER A STAKE OR USING DULL KNIVES.

NATIVE AMERICAN CRAFTS ARE A NATURAL PART OF OUR HERITAGE THAT WE ALL SHOULD BE PROUD OF AND LEARN TO APPRECIATE.

NATURAL FOODS

MANY OF OUR TRADITIONAL FOODS WERE ORIGINATED BY THE INDIAN WOMAN. FOR INSTANCE, CORNBREAD, BAKED BEANS, AND EVEN THAT POPULAR SUBURBAN STYLE OF COOKING WE CALL THE BARBEQUE.

NATIVE AMERICAN MOCCASINS ARE ONE OF THE MOST COMFORTABLE AND PRACTICAL KINDS OF FOOTWEAR. THEY ARE ALSO EASY AND FUN TO MAKE. THE IDEAL LEATHER FOR MOCCASINS IS "HOME-TANNED" BUCKSKIN; HOWEVER A GOOD SUBSTITUTE CAN BE HAD FROM SEVERAL LEATHER COMPANIES. (CHECK WITH LOCAL CRAFTS SHOPS.)

1. THE FIRST STEP IS TO MAKE A PATTERN OF YOUR FOOT. FOLD A PAPER IN HALF, PLACE YOUR FOOT ON IT AND DRAW AROUND THE FRONT OF YOUR FOOT - BACK TO THE WIDEST PART OF YOUR FOOT. THEN DRAW A LINE PARALLEL TO THE FOLDED EDGE. *THE LINE AROUND YOUR TOES SHOULD BE 3/4 INCH AWAY FROM YOUR FOOT.* CUT OUT THE PAPER PATTERN, LEAVING AT LEAST 1-INCH EXCESS AT THE HEEL.

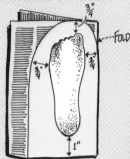

2. OPEN THE PATTERN AND MARK AND CUT LINES XX AND YY. LINE XX IS LOCATED WHERE YOUR FOOT IS WIDEST, AND APPROXIMATELY 1-INCH LESS IN LENGTH THAN THE WIDTH OF YOUR FOOT. MAKE A RIGHT AND LEFT-HAND PATTERN, THEN TRACE ONTO LEATHER USING A BALL POINT PEN.

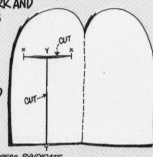

©1972 UNIVERSAL PRESS SYNDICATE

3. CUT OUT MOCCASINS AND SEW THE OUTSIDE EDGES TOGETHER. MOCCASIN IS WRONG SIDE OUT AT THIS TIME. TO SEW LEATHER PROPERLY, YOU SHOULD PUNCH HOLES THROUGH THE LEATHER WITH A SHARP AWL BEFORE STITCHING. HOLES SHOULD BE 1/8 INCH APART AND 1/8 INCH FROM THE EDGE. PUNCH ONLY A FEW HOLES AT A TIME. THE MOCCASINS SHOULD BE SEWN WITH SHOE-MAKERS' THREAD AND A LARGE NEEDLE. *KEEP THE THREAD WAXED WITH BEESWAX.*

4. REVERSE THE MOCCASINS TO RIGHT SIDE OUT AND CUT THE INSIDE LINES.

5. CUT A 2 x 3½ INCH TONGUE AND SEW IT IN PLACE.

6. PLACE MOCCASIN ON FOOT, PINCH BACK TOGETHER TO DETERMINE LENGTH. CUT OFF SURPLUS AND STITCH UP. CUT IN ON LINE X AND STITCH THIS BOTTOM FLAP UP IN PLACE. CUT ½ INCH WIDE SLITS AROUND THE SIDES FOR TIE THONGS, AND THREAD RAWHIDE THROUGH THEM.

Natural Crafts

IF YOU WISH TO DECORATE YOUR MOCCASINS YOU MIGHT TRY BEADING THEM IN AN AUTHENTIC STYLE. (BEADS ARE AVAILABLE AT CRAFT SHOPS.)

TWO THREADS ARE USED TO BEAD MOCCASINS. ONE THREAD IS USED TO HOLD THE BEADS - THE OTHER TO STITCH THE BEADED THREAD IN PLACE.

SOME TRADITIONAL DESIGNS

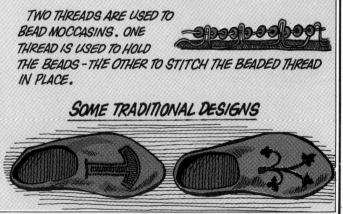

NATURAL DYE SOURCES

RED: Pokeberry Berries
BROWN: Black Walnut Hulls
GREEN: Staghorn Sumac Leaves, Twigs, Seeds
YELLOW: Dandelion Flowers
BLUE: Elderberry Berries

NATURAL FOODS

SASSAFRAS TEA - A VERY PLEASANT BEVERAGE MADE BY BOILING ROOTS OR BARK OF SASSAFRAS TREE WAS CONSIDERED A NECESSARY "SPRING TONIC," AND WAS USED TO LOSE WEIGHT AND TO KEEP THIN. IT IS NOW CONSIDERED TOXIC.

BUCK-BRUSH "INDIAN CURRANT" PLANT WAS A PLANT VALUED BY THE FIRST AMERICANS. THE TOUGH-WOODY ROOTS CAN BE MADE INTO BASKETS, THE BERRIES WERE USED IN "INDIAN PEMMICAN," A TYPE OF DRIED MEAT. TODAY IT'S ONE PLANT THAT SEES MANY BIRDS AND ANIMALS THROUGH ROUGH WINTERS.

Dye Sources

RED   BROWN   GREEN

BLUE   YELLOW

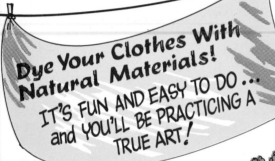

Dye Your Clothes With Natural Materials!

IT'S FUN AND EASY TO DO... and YOU'LL BE PRACTICING A TRUE ART!

1. GATHER MATERIALS NEEDED; BERRIES, TWIGS, LEAVES, FLOWERS.

2. CRUSH MATERIALS AND BOIL FOR AT LEAST 2 HOURS, STRAIN.

3. WASH FABRIC IN BOILING "SOFT" OR RAINWATER WITH PLENTY OF SOAP, THEN RINSE.

4. PLACE WET FABRIC IN WARM DYE BATH. RAISE DYE TEMPERATURE TO 200° F. AND MAINTAIN HEAT FOR 30 MINUTES – OR UNTIL DESIRED COLOR IS ATTAINED.

5. RINSE DYED MATERIALS AT LEAST THREE TIMES.

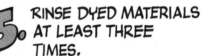

6. DRY INDOORS OR IN THE SHADE.

To make your dyes more color-fast, add Alum to dye bath.

Natural Crafts

TIE DYEING is an easy, enjoyable way of dyeing very unusual patterns.

A variety of materials lend themselves to the techniques of TIE DYEING –

1. GATHER MATERIAL INTO "BALLS"; TIE TIGHTLY WITH STRING.

2. PREPARE DYE BATH AND DYE TIED CLOTH IN THE NORMAL MANNER.

3. RETIE DIFFERENT AREAS FOR ADDING OTHER COLORS.

8
SPORTS

AND HOBBIES

ARCHERY IS ONE OF MAN'S OLDEST SPORTS.

NATURAL FOODS

VENISON IS THE OBJECT OF THE GAME TO MOST "BOWHUNTERS" AND, IF TREATED and PREPARED PROPERLY, CAN BE AS DELICIOUS AS THE BEST "CORN-FED" BEEF. VENISON STEAKS ARE GREAT COOKED USING YOUR FAVORITE "BARBECUE" SAUCE. ALL FAT SHOULD BE REMOVED FROM VENISON, and IT SHOULD BE TURNED EVERY 5 TO 10 MINUTES TO KEEP IN THE JUICES.

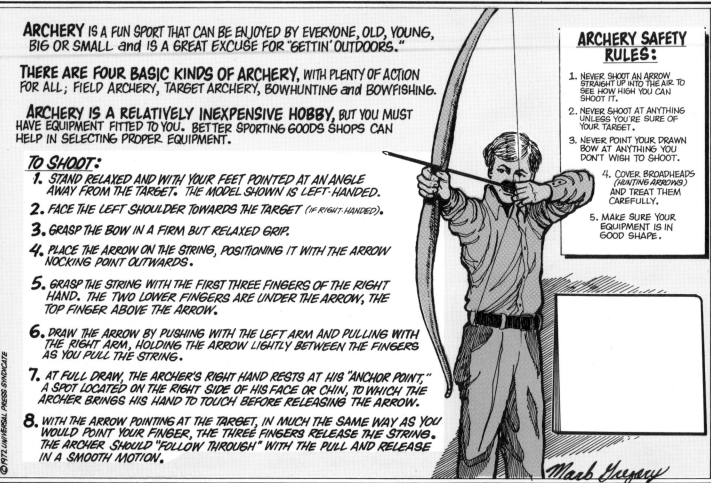

ARCHERY IS A FUN SPORT THAT CAN BE ENJOYED BY EVERYONE, OLD, YOUNG, BIG OR SMALL and IS A GREAT EXCUSE FOR "GETTIN' OUTDOORS."

THERE ARE FOUR BASIC KINDS OF ARCHERY, WITH PLENTY OF ACTION FOR ALL; FIELD ARCHERY, TARGET ARCHERY, BOWHUNTING and BOWFISHING.

ARCHERY IS A RELATIVELY INEXPENSIVE HOBBY, BUT YOU MUST HAVE EQUIPMENT FITTED TO YOU. BETTER SPORTING GOODS SHOPS CAN HELP IN SELECTING PROPER EQUIPMENT.

TO SHOOT:

1. STAND RELAXED AND WITH YOUR FEET POINTED AT AN ANGLE AWAY FROM THE TARGET. THE MODEL SHOWN IS LEFT-HANDED.

2. FACE THE LEFT SHOULDER TOWARDS THE TARGET (IF RIGHT-HANDED).

3. GRASP THE BOW IN A FIRM BUT RELAXED GRIP.

4. PLACE THE ARROW ON THE STRING, POSITIONING IT WITH THE ARROW NOCKING POINT OUTWARDS.

5. GRASP THE STRING WITH THE FIRST THREE FINGERS OF THE RIGHT HAND. THE TWO LOWER FINGERS ARE UNDER THE ARROW, THE TOP FINGER ABOVE THE ARROW.

6. DRAW THE ARROW BY PUSHING WITH THE LEFT ARM AND PULLING WITH THE RIGHT ARM, HOLDING THE ARROW LIGHTLY BETWEEN THE FINGERS AS YOU PULL THE STRING.

7. AT FULL DRAW, THE ARCHER'S RIGHT HAND RESTS AT HIS "ANCHOR POINT," A SPOT LOCATED ON THE RIGHT SIDE OF HIS FACE OR CHIN, TO WHICH THE ARCHER BRINGS HIS HAND TO TOUCH BEFORE RELEASING THE ARROW.

8. WITH THE ARROW POINTING AT THE TARGET, IN MUCH THE SAME WAY AS YOU WOULD POINT YOUR FINGER, THE THREE FINGERS RELEASE THE STRING. THE ARCHER SHOULD "FOLLOW THROUGH" WITH THE PULL AND RELEASE IN A SMOOTH MOTION.

ARCHERY SAFETY RULES:

1. NEVER SHOOT AN ARROW STRAIGHT UP INTO THE AIR TO SEE HOW HIGH YOU CAN SHOOT IT.

2. NEVER SHOOT AT ANYTHING UNLESS YOU'RE SURE OF YOUR TARGET.

3. NEVER POINT YOUR DRAWN BOW AT ANYTHING YOU DON'T WISH TO SHOOT.

4. COVER BROADHEADS (HUNTING ARROWS) AND TREAT THEM CAREFULLY.

5. MAKE SURE YOUR EQUIPMENT IS IN GOOD SHAPE.

Mark Gregory

Natural Crafts

YOU CAN EASILY MAKE YOUR OWN "TARGET" OR ARROW BACKSTOPS. MERELY PLACE FOUR BALES OF STRAW IN A STACK ON THEIR SIDES. PLACE THE PAPER TARGET OVER THE STRAW, PINNING IT IN PLACE TO THE STRAW WITH SHARPENED STICKS.

--OR--

YOU CAN MAKE YOUR OWN BACKSTOPS FROM BOXES STUFFED WITH DISCARDED NEWSPAPERS OR MAGAZINES.

PAINT ON YOUR OWN BULLS-EYE.

A GOOD, SAFE DETERRENT FOR PESKY DOGS WHILE CAMPING or BICYCLING IS A TOY WATER PISTOL FILLED WITH WATER.

NATURAL FOODS

A GOOD QUICK-ENERGY FOOD FOR BICYCLING and CAMPING IS A HOME-MADE CANDY BAR OF SALTED PEANUTS AND RAISINS COVERED WITH YOUR FAVORITE KIND OF CHOCOLATE.

BICYCLE TOURING

OR CAMPING IS A FUN AND GREAT WAY TO TRAVEL, AND IS BECOMING INCREASINGLY POPULAR THROUGHOUT THE COUNTRY.

BICYCLE "TRIPPING" CAN BE AS SIMPLE OR CHALLENGING AS YOU LIKE -- THE BICYCLER CAN STAY AT MOTELS, EAT AT RESTAURANTS, JUST AS IN AUTO CAMPING, OR CAN CARRY HIS OWN FOOD AND GEAR JUST AS IN BACKPACKING, STAYING IN THE NUMEROUS STATE, NATIONAL and PRIVATE CAMPING PARKS. MANY NATIONAL PARKS AND STATE PARKS HAVE SPECIAL AREAS WITH TRAILS MARKED, SET ASIDE FOR BICYCLE CAMPERS.

THE FIRST PREREQUISITE IS A BICYCLE, AND FOR TRIPS OF ANY LENGTH, YOU'LL WANT A GOOD MULTI-GEAR TOURING BIKE. THESE ARE CALLED "DERAILLEUR" BICYCLES, AND ARE EXTREMELY LIGHTWEIGHT, HAVE A GOOD LUGGAGE RACK, 2 HAND BRAKES AND POSSIBLY SADDLE (PANNIER) BAGS ATTACHED OVER THE REAR TIRE. A CHILD'S SEAT CAN BE ATTACHED FRONT OR BACK FOR CARRYING YOUNG CHILDREN.

MAKE SURE THAT A REPAIR KIT IS ALSO ATTACHED, AND INCLUDES: SPARE TIRES and TUBES, TIRE PUMP, TUBE PATCHING KIT, MASTER CHAIN LINK, CHAIN OIL, ADJUSTABLE WRENCH, SCREWDRIVER, PLIERS, POCKET KNIFE, AS WELL AS EXTRA HUB NUTS, VALVE STEM, BRAKE BLOCKS and CABLE.

© 1972 UNIVERSAL PRESS SYNDICATE

BICYCLE TRIPPING IS ONLY AS SAFE AS THE ABILITIES OF THE INDIVIDUAL RIDERS -- BUT CERTAIN SAFETY RULES SHOULD BE OBSERVED.
1. WATCH FOR ROAD HAZARDS
2. DON'T USE BRAKES CONTINUOUSLY ON DOWNHILL RUNS -- YOU MAY DAMAGE THEM.
3. PROCEED DOWNHILL AS SLOWLY AS POSSIBLE
4. KEEP INSIDE PEDAL UP DURING TURNS
5. USE HAND SIGNALS
6. WATCH FOR AUTOMOBILES
7. WEAR BRIGHT COLORS
8. DON'T RIDE AT NIGHT

IF YOU'RE STAYING AT MOTELS and EATING AT RESTAURANTS, YOU CAN GO EXTREMELY LIGHT, CARRYING ONLY YOUR CLOTHES PLUS A LIGHTWEIGHT RAINSUIT.

IF YOU'RE CAMPING YOU WILL NEED: A LIGHTWEIGHT SLEEPING BAG, (A 3-POUND BAG WILL SUFFICE FOR MOST SUMMER CAMPING) A SMALL ALUMINUM NESTED COOKING KIT, SMALL ALCOHOL or SOLID FUEL STOVE, LIGHTWEIGHT MOUNTAIN or PLASTIC TUBE TENT, AND NATURALLY FOOD. ALTHOUGH SOMEWHAT EXPENSIVE, THE FREEZE-DRIED BACK-PACKING FOODS AVAILABLE THROUGH MOST CAMPING STORES WILL PROVIDE A WELL-BALANCED DIET WITH THE LEAST AMOUNT OF EFFORT.

FOR MORE INFORMATION ON CLUBS and TOURING TRAILS IN THE U.S.A. or CANADA WRITE: AMERICAN YOUTH HOSTELS, INC. NATIONAL HEADQUARTERS 20 W. 17TH ST. NEW YORK, NY 10011

Natural Crafts

A HANDY COMBINATION PONCHO-TENT CAN BE MADE FROM AN 8 x 8 FT. SECTION OF LIGHTWEIGHT COATED-NYLON.

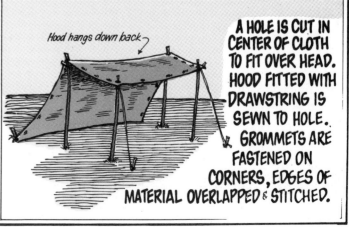

Hood hangs down back

A HOLE IS CUT IN CENTER OF CLOTH TO FIT OVER HEAD. HOOD FITTED WITH DRAWSTRING IS SEWN TO HOLE. GROMMETS ARE FASTENED ON CORNERS, EDGES OF MATERIAL OVERLAPPED & STITCHED.

SOLITARY BIRD WATCHING GIVES A PERSON TIME FOR SOME QUIET THOUGHTS.

SUPPORT CONSERVATION CLUBS SUCH AS THE AUDUBON SOCIETY, WILDERNESS SOCIETY, NATIONAL WILDLIFE and DUCKS UNLIMITED WHO ARE FIGHTING TO PRESERVE BIRD and ANIMAL HABITAT.

BIRD WATCHING, A FUN HOBBY THAT IS MANY TIMES UNCONSCIOUSLY PRACTICED BY EXPERIENCED WOODSMEN, IS A FUN AND EDUCATIONAL ACTIVITY THAT CAN BE ENJOYED BY ALMOST ANYONE OF ANY AGE. AND IT CAN BE DONE ALONE, WITH YOUR FAMILY, OR A LARGE GROUP.

THE FIRST REQUIREMENT IS A GOOD FIELD GUIDE IDENTIFICATION TO BIRDS, SUCH AS PETERSONS, OR THE GOLDEN FIELD GUIDE (available at local bookstores). YOU MAY ALSO WISH TO ADD A GOOD PAIR OF BINOCULARS TO AID IN SEEING WARY OR SMALL BIRDS MORE CLEARLY. A 7×35 BINOCULAR IS FAVORED BY MANY BIRDWATCHERS.

THE GREAT THING ABOUT BIRD WATCHING IS THAT YOU CAN ENJOY IT IN YOUR OWN BACKYARD, OR SOME REMOTE JUNGLE OR MOUNTAIN FOREST.

SETTING UP A FEEDING STATION OR BIRD-BATH IN YOUR BACKYARD WILL HELP BRING IN MORE BIRDS. LOCATE THESE OUT IN THE OPEN AND HIGH ENOUGH ABOVE THE GROUND TO DISCOURAGE CATS AND DOGS.

ONE WAY OF DRAWING BIRDS CLOSER FOR OBSERVATION IS TO LEARN THEIR CALLS AND TRY TO CALL THEM. IT'S EXACTING TO LEARN AND A TRULY EXCITING SPORT.

OTHER EXCELLENT PLACES FOR BIRD WATCHERS ARE THE NATIONAL FORESTS AND NATIONAL AND STATE PARKS. EXCELLENT BIRD WATCHING FOR SOME EXCITING BIRDS IS AVAILABLE EACH YEAR IN THE NUMEROUS WATERFOWL REFUGES SCATTERED AROUND THE UNITED STATES AND CANADA. (BEFORE OR AFTER THE WATERFOWL SEASON.)

ONE EXCELLENT PLACE, AND OFTEN OVERLOOKED BY MANY, IS THE BACK-COUNTRY ROADS. IF YOU DRIVE THESE OLD GRAVEL AND DIRT ROADS SLOWLY AND CAUTIOUSLY, YOU'LL SEE HUNDREDS OF BIRDS.

WHEN YOU'RE TRYING TO OBSERVE WARY WILD BIRDS YOU'LL HAVE TO LEARN TO "CAMOUFLAGE" YOURSELF TO BLEND IN WITH THE BACKGROUND. WEARING A CAMOUFLAGE SUIT IS ONE GOOD WAY OF DOING THIS. THIS IS OBVIOUSLY NOT A GOOD IDEA, HOWEVER, DURING PEAK HUNTING SEASONS OR IN AREAS FREQUENTED BY HUNTERS.

Mark Gregory

Natural Crafts

START A LIFE LIST OR LIST OF BIRDS YOU HAVE IDENTIFIED AND ADD TO IT WITH EACH NEW BIRD.

THE LIFE LIST SHOULD STATE THE LOCATION AT WHICH THE BIRD WAS SEEN, THE TIME OF DAY and THE DATE, AS WELL AS NAME OF BIRD AND ACTIVITY.

NAME _____
LOCATION _____
TIME _____
DATE _____
COMMENTS _____

SLIPPING QUIETLY DOWN A SLOW BACKWATER STREAM IN A CANOE IS AN EXCELLENT WAY TO SEE WILDLIFE SUCH AS BEAVER, DEER, SQUIRRELS and HUNDREDS OF BIRDS.

NATURAL FOODS

FOR AN UNUSUAL and HEALTHFUL SNACK TRY ROASTED SOYBEANS.

SOAK BEANS IN SALT WATER OVERNIGHT, THEN BOIL FOR AN HOUR. SPREAD BEANS OUT IN SHALLOW PANS AND ROAST IN A 350° OVEN UNTIL BROWN.

SALT TO TASTE.

CANOEING IS AN EXCELLENT SPORT THAT THE ENTIRE FAMILY CAN ENJOY. AND IT DOESN'T REQUIRE YEARS OF EXPERIENCE. A FEW MINUTES PRACTICE IN SOME QUIET BACKWATER and YOU'LL BE PADDLING WELL ENOUGH TO KEEP YOURSELF HEADED IN THE RIGHT DIRECTION.

DON'T TACKLE FAST WATER AND TRICKY STREAMS UNTIL YOU'VE MASTERED THE ART OF PADDLING. IT'S WISE TO RENT A CANOE FOR YOUR FIRST FEW TRIPS, THEN YOU CAN DETERMINE WHAT SIZE and TYPE YOU MAY WISH TO BUY.

PADDLES ARE USED TO PROPEL THE CANOE and/or GUIDE IT THROUGH THE WATER. THE STERN (rear) MAN'S PADDLE SHOULD BE LONG ENOUGH TO REACH HIS EYES WHEN HE IS STANDING. THE BOW (front) MAN'S PADDLE SHOULD BE ABOUT 3 INCHES SHORTER, or REACHING TO ABOUT HIS CHIN.

THESE ARE THE BASIC STROKES USED BY BOTH STERN and BOW PADDLERS:

POWER STROKE: THE CANOER THRUSTS THE PADDLE INTO THE WATER and PULLS BACK WITH HIS LOWER HAND, PUSHING FORWARD WITH HIS UPPER HAND.

STEERING STROKE: WHEN THE BOW and STERN PADDLERS ARE PADDLING ON OPPOSITE SIDES THE BASIC STEERING STROKE IS STARTED JUST AS THE POWER STROKE, BUT AT THE LAST MOMENT THE BLADE IS TURNED SIDEWAYS and PUSHED AWAY FROM THE CANOE CAUSING THE REAR OF CANOE TO MOVE SIDEWAYS.

BACKWATER STROKE: TO DECREASE SPEED or CAUSE THE CANOE TO TURN IN RAPIDS, THE PADDLE IS HELD FIRMLY IN POSITION IN THE WATER, CAUSING A DRAG ON THAT SIDE OF THE CANOE.

TWO PEOPLE IN A CANOE REQUIRE TEAMWORK. THE BOW PADDLER'S JOB IS TO WATCH OUT FOR OBSTACLES, and TO PADDLE THE CANOE FORWARD WHEN REQUIRED.

THE STERN PADDLER MUST WATCH THE BOW PADDLER and KEEP HIS PADDLE ON THE OPPOSITE SIDE OF THE CANOE TO COUNTERACT THE TENDENCY OF THE CANOE TO TURN WITH THE BOW PADDLER.

THE STERN PADDLER'S MOST IMPORTANT JOB IS STEERING.

ALWAYS WEAR AN APPROVED LIFE JACKET WHEN CANOEING.

Mark Gregory

Natural Crafts

AN EXCELLENT WATERPROOF CASE TO USE WHEN CANOEING. TO HOLD YOUR CAMERAS and VALUABLES CAN BE MADE FROM AN EMPTY ARMY AMMO BOX. (AVAILABLE AT ARMY SURPLUS or CAMPING SUPPLY STORES.)

1. LINE INSIDE OF BOX WITH FOAM RUBBER.

2. PAINT OUTSIDE WITH ALUMINUM PAINT TO KEEP INSIDE COOL. CHAIN BOX TO CANOE USING AN OLD DOG LEASH.

WALK AS MUCH AS POSSIBLE, USE YOUR AUTOMOBILE ONLY WHEN ABSOLUTELY NECESSARY, AND THE WHOLE WORLD WILL BE HEALTHIER.

NATURAL FOODS

FOOD FOR HIKING MUST BE LIGHTWEIGHT, YET QUICK ENERGY GIVING. FOR SHORT TRIPS CARRY A PACKAGE OF JERKY, DRIED FRUIT OR, IN COOL WEATHER, CHOCOLATE BARS.

HIKING AMERICA'S TRAILS and FOOTPATHS IS A HOBBY THAT HAS MANY REWARDS -- FRESH AIR, HEALTHFUL EXERCISE, HISTORIC KNOW-LEDGE, BUT THE BEST OF ALL, A SENSE OF BELONGING THAT COMES ONLY FROM MEETING THE OUTDOORS CLOSE-UP AND IN HER OWN "BACKYARD."

NOW IS THE TIME TO START PLANNING FOR YOUR SUMMER TRIP. THERE ARE THOUSANDS OF MILES OF PLANNED, MARKED TRAILS SCATTERED ALL OVER THE UNITED STATES, AND MANY THOUSANDS MORE IN THE PLANNING AND DEVELOPMENT STAGE. THIS INCLUDES SUCH HISTORIC AND FAR REACHING TRAILS AS THE SANTA FE, AS WELL AS METROPOLITAN "LOOP" AND NATURE TRAILS, AND THE SHORT NATURE TRAILS THROUGH MANY NATIONAL PARKS.

HIKING TRIPS CAN BE ANYTHING FROM A MONTH-LONG BACKPACKING TRIP THROUGH EXPANSIVE WILDERNESS TO A SHORT HIKE DOWN A RAVINE FOR A CLOSER LOOK AT A BEAUTIFUL WATERFALL OR OTHER NATURAL WONDER IN A WELL DEVELOPED NATIONAL PARK.

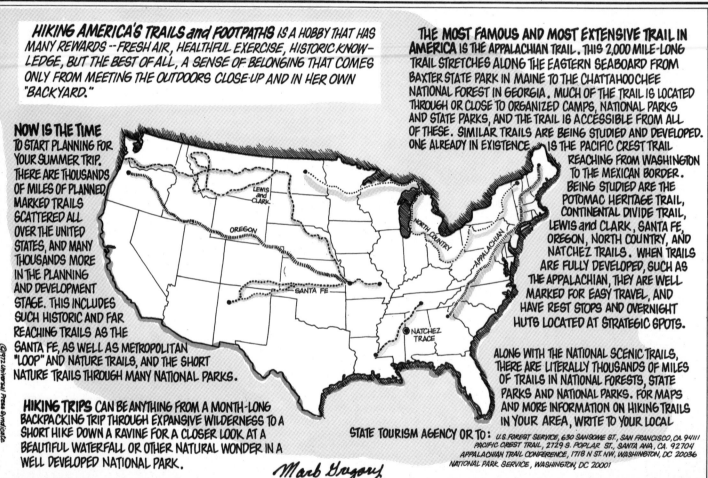

©1972 Universal Press Syndicate

THE MOST FAMOUS AND MOST EXTENSIVE TRAIL IN AMERICA IS THE APPALACHIAN TRAIL. THIS 2,000 MILE-LONG TRAIL STRETCHES ALONG THE EASTERN SEABOARD FROM BAXTER STATE PARK IN MAINE TO THE CHATTAHOOCHEE NATIONAL FOREST IN GEORGIA. MUCH OF THE TRAIL IS LOCATED THROUGH OR CLOSE TO ORGANIZED CAMPS, NATIONAL PARKS AND STATE PARKS, AND THE TRAIL IS ACCESSIBLE FROM ALL OF THESE. SIMILAR TRAILS ARE BEING STUDIED AND DEVELOPED. ONE ALREADY IN EXISTENCE IS THE PACIFIC CREST TRAIL REACHING FROM WASHINGTON TO THE MEXICAN BORDER. BEING STUDIED ARE THE POTOMAC HERITAGE TRAIL, CONTINENTAL DIVIDE TRAIL, LEWIS and CLARK, SANTA FE, OREGON, NORTH COUNTRY, AND NATCHEZ TRAILS. WHEN TRAILS ARE FULLY DEVELOPED, SUCH AS THE APPALACHIAN, THEY ARE WELL MARKED FOR EASY TRAVEL, AND HAVE REST STOPS AND OVERNIGHT HUTS LOCATED AT STRATEGIC SPOTS.

ALONG WITH THE NATIONAL SCENIC TRAILS, THERE ARE LITERALLY THOUSANDS OF MILES OF TRAILS IN NATIONAL FORESTS, STATE PARKS AND NATIONAL PARKS. FOR MAPS AND MORE INFORMATION ON HIKING TRAILS IN YOUR AREA, WRITE TO YOUR LOCAL STATE TOURISM AGENCY OR TO: U.S. FOREST SERVICE, 630 SANSOME ST., SAN FRANCISCO, CA. 94111 PACIFIC CREST TRAIL, 2729 S. POPLAR ST., SANTA ANA, CA. 92704 APPALACHIAN TRAIL CONFERENCE, 1718 N ST. NW, WASHINGTON, DC 20036 NATIONAL PARK SERVICE, WASHINGTON, DC 20001

Marb Gregory

Natural Crafts

THE SINGLE MOST IMPORTANT ITEM OF THE "WALKER" IS A GOOD PAIR OF **HIKING BOOTS**. THESE SHOULD BE ABOUT A HALF-SIZE LARGER THAN YOUR NORMAL SHOE SIZE TO ACCOMODATE YOUR FEET AS THEY SWELL DURING AN EXTENDED HIKE. WEAR TWO PAIRS OF WOOL SOCKS.

A STURDY "STAFF" IS A GREAT HELP FOR ANY WALKER. THE STAFF MAKES A THIRD LEG FOR BETTER BALANCE ON HILL-SIDES, WHEN FORDING STREAMS, AND IT'S HANDY FOR SCARING OFF OVERBRAVE DOGS.

9

WORKING
WITH NATURE

BIRDS ARE A GOOD FRIEND TO MAN.

NATURAL FOODS

WHEN BIRDS HAVE THEIR OWN FOODS THEY WILL LEAVE THE TAMER CROPS (yours) ALONE.

IF YOU WANT TO ENJOY MORE BIRDS AROUND YOUR PROPERTY, PLANT TO ATTRACT THEM.

THE PLANTS YOU CHOOSE SHOULD FULFILL THESE REQUIREMENTS:

1. THEY SHOULD FURNISH FOOD OR SHELTER TO BIRDS, PREFERABLY YEAR-ROUND. (CHOOSING A GOOD VARIETY OF PLANTS WILL HELP INSURE YEAR-ROUND FOOD AND SHELTER.)

2. PLANTS SHOULD PROVIDE GOOD NESTING SITES AND PROTECTION FROM PREDATORS.

3. PICK PLANTS THAT WILL IMPROVE THE APPEARANCE OF YOUR PROPERTY.

4. PICK PLANTS THAT ARE EASY TO CARE FOR AND MAINTAIN.

THESE ARE SOME OF THE TREES AND SHRUBS FAVORED BY BIRDS:

RED CEDARS: THIS IS ONE OF THE BEST PLANTS FOR ANY KIND OF BIRD OR ANIMAL HABITAT IMPROVEMENT. THEY GROW FAST AND PROVIDE PLENTY OF FOOD AND SHELTER, EVEN DURING WINTER STORMS.

OTHER TREES INCLUDE: **REDBUDS, DOGWOODS, OAKS, WALNUTS, ETC.**

A GOOD HEDGE MADE UP OF A VARIETY OF PLANTS WILL ALSO BE A GREAT ATTRACTOR. PLANTS SUCH AS **CURRANTS, BLUEBERRIES, HIGHBUSH CRANBERRIES, SPICEBUSH** and **MULTIFLOWER ROSE** MAKE AN EXCELLENT HEDGE.

GOOD CLIMBING VINES ARE **HONEYSUCKLE** AND **VIRGINIA CREEPER.**

BY CREATING BETTER HABITAT, YOU CAN ALMOST DOUBLE THE BIRD POPULATION IN YOUR AREA.

Mark Gregory

Natural Crafts

PLANTING CEDARS AS "SHELTER BELTS" IS A GOOD WAY OF BENEFITING BOTH THE BIRDS and YOURSELF.

PLANT TREES TO STOP NORTH WINDS OR DRIFTING SNOW.

PROVIDING THE PROPER FEED FOR WILD MIGRATING GEESE IS A GROWING NATIONAL PROBLEM. WILD GEESE DEPEND HEAVILY ON GRAIN, AND THE WILDLIFE REFUGES ACROSS THE COUNTRY FEED TONS OF CORN, WHEAT AND RICE TO THE MILLIONS OF MIGRATING DUCKS AND GEESE.

NATURAL FOODS

WHILE YOU'RE BUYING GRAINS FOR YOUR BIRDS, BUY SOME FOR YOURSELF! NOTHING BEATS HOT HOME-MADE BREAD, ESPECIALLY WHEN IT'S MADE OF 100% WHOLE WHEAT FLOUR FROM GRAIN YOU'VE GROUND YOURSELF. WHOLE WHEAT BREAD IS ALSO BETTER FOR YOU. IT DOESN'T LOSE THE WHEAT GERM AND VITAMINS E and B IN PROCESSING. IF YOU DON'T WISH TO GRIND YOUR OWN GRAIN, YOU CAN BUY WHOLE WHEAT FLOUR FROM MANY GROCERS or ORGANIC FOOD STORES.

FEEDING WILD BIRDS

CAN BE A <u>YEAR ROUND</u> HOBBY ENJOYED BY EVERYONE IN YOUR FAMILY. BUILD OR PURCHASE A FEEDER FOR YOUR WINDOWSILL OR GARDEN AND KEEP IT FILLED WITH NATURAL FOODS OR THOSE THAT BIRDS WOULD CHOOSE FOR THEMSELVES. THE BIRDS WILL IN TURN PROVIDE YOU AND YOUR CHILDREN WITH MANY HOURS OF ENJOYMENT AND EDUCATION.

Natural Bird Foods:

1. Berries 2. Nuts
3. Wild cherries 4. Weed seeds
5. Crab apples

YOU CAN PICK THESE ITEMS AND STORE THEM IN SHALLOW TRAYS IN A DARK, DRY PLACE, OR PACKED LOOSELY IN AN OLD NYLON HOSE FOR USE IN THE WINTER.

IF YOU WISH TO PURCHASE BIRD FOOD -BUY WHOLE GRAINS (CORN, WHEAT, RICE, MILLET) FROM A GRAIN AND FEED STORE OR NATURAL FOOD STORE.

IF YOU CAN'T FIND BERRIES OR NUTS DURING THE WINTER MONTHS, You can usually find weed seeds on dried up weeds along the roadside or in vacant lots. Whichever weed seeds are the most common in your area will be those used by the birds. Some common favorites might be foxtails, ragweed, wild mustard, etc.

WARNING: ONCE YOU START PUTTING OUT FOOD, YOU MUST KEEP IT UP, BECAUSE THE BIRDS BEGIN TO DEPEND ON YOU. IN PARTS OF THE COUNTRY WHICH HAVE SEVERE WINTER MONTHS, A SMALL BIRD CAN DIE IN A LITTLE OVER A DAY WITHOUT FOOD.

SOME BIRDS PREFER SCRAPS OF MEAT. FOR THESE BIRDS PLACE RAW MEAT TRIMMINGS (from your steak or hamburger) ON TREE LIMBS OR IN THE FEEDER.

Always provide water as well as food.

AN OLD GARBAGE CAN LID PLACED ON A COUPLE OF BRICKS WILL SERVE AS AN EXCELLENT BIRD BATH AND WATER HOLE.

Natural Crafts

YOU CAN EASILY MAKE YOUR OWN BIRD FEEDERS. SHOWN HERE ARE TWO EASILY CONSTRUCTED TYPES OF FEEDERS.

AN UNUSUAL FEEDER FOR WOODPECKERS IS A SUSPENDED LOG WITH HOLES BORED IN IT AND STUFFED WITH MEAT SCRAPS.

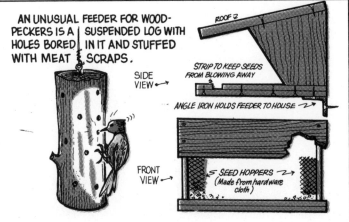

ROOF
STRIP TO KEEP SEEDS FROM BLOWING AWAY
SIDE VIEW
ANGLE IRON HOLDS FEEDER TO HOUSE
FRONT VIEW
SEED HOPPERS (Made from hardware cloth)

91

CHRISTMAS TREE FARM

NATURAL CHRISTMAS TREES ARE AN EASILY RENEWABLE RESOURCE.

NATURAL FOODS

THE INDIANS AND EARLY SETTLERS MADE AN INVIGORATING, IF SOMEWHAT BITTER, TEA BY BOILING WHITE-PINE NEEDLES IN WATER.

WHEN YOU TAKE DOWN THAT BEAUTIFULLY-DECORATED NATURAL PINE OR CEDAR CHRISTMAS TREE IT BECOMES A SOURCE OF POLLUTION. INSTEAD OF THROWING YOUR CHRISTMAS TREE OUT THE FRONT DOOR WHERE IT BECOMES A PROBLEM FOR THE TRASH PICKUP MAN, "GIVE IT BACK TO NATURE." DISCARDED CHRISTMAS TREES USED PROPERLY CAN BE A REAL BENEFIT TO ALL KINDS OF WILDLIFE.

HERE ARE SOME OF THE WAYS DISCARDED CHRISTMAS TREES CAN BE "RECYCLED."

1. TIED IN BUNDLES, WITH A COUPLE OF HEAVY ROCKS TIED TO THEM, AND DROPPED IN YOUR FAVORITE FISHING HOLE, POND OR LAKE, THEY PROVIDE EXCELLENT "CRAPPIE BEDS," AND BASS HIDING PLACES. (MAKE SURE YOU OBTAIN PERMISSION FROM THE OWNER, BUT IN ALL LIKELIHOOD HE'LL WELCOME YOU WITH YOUR TREES, AS WELL AS NEXT SUMMER WHEN YOU'RE LOOKING FOR A SPOT TO TAKE YOUR SON OR DAUGHTER "BLUEGILL FISHING.")

THIS IS THE BEST TIME OF THE YEAR TO "PLANT" UNDERWATER BRUSHPILES BECAUSE YOU CAN MERELY DRAG THE TREES OUT ON FROZEN ICE TO WHERE YOU WANT THEM AND LEAVE THEM.

2. ANOTHER EXCELLENT WAY TO USE CHRISTMAS TREES IS TO PILE THEM IN CORNERS OF FIELDS, OR ALONG FENCE ROWS TO MAKE COVER BRUSH PILES FOR QUAIL, PHEASANTS, RABBITS AND LOTS OF OTHER WILDLIFE.

3. ONE GOOD OLD-TIME WAY OF DISPOSING OF ALL KINDS OF UNWANTED BRUSH, INCLUDING USED CHRISTMAS TREES, IS TO PILE THEM INTO A GULLEY TO STOP EROSION. IN A COUPLE OF YEARS THE GULLEY WILL BE FULL OF VEGETATION AND THE WATER RUN-OFF WILL HAVE BEEN SLOWED DOWN. THESE GULLEYS ARE ALSO EMERGENCY HOMES FOR WILDLIFE DURING EXTREMELY HARD WINTER STORMS.

IF YOU REALLY WANT TO HELP, START A NEIGHBORHOOD DRIVE AND GATHER UP AS MANY TREES AS YOU CAN.

Mack Gregory

Natural Crafts

IF YOU'RE AN ORGANIC GARDENER, OR HAVE A FRIEND WHO IS, CHRISTMAS TREES ARE A "BONUS." RUN THEM THROUGH A SHREDDER AND ADD THEM TO THE COMPOST PILE.

CHRISTMAS WREATHS AND OTHER NATURAL DECORATIONS MAY ALSO BE "USED" IN THE SAME MANNER AS CHRISTMAS TREES, BUT MAKE SURE YOU REMOVE ALL NON-ORGANIC MATERIALS BEFORE DISCARDING.

WOOD IS MAN'S MOST VALUABLE RESOURCE.
IT IS A LIVING, RENEWABLE RESOURCE THAT CAN BE AS "IMMORTAL" AS MAN ALLOWS.

NATURAL FOODS

YOU CAN EASILY MAKE OLD-FASHIONED NATURAL COTTAGE CHEESE. WARM A QUART OF SOURED or "CLABBERED" MILK TO WRIST TEMPERATURE. Place the warmed curds in a cheesecloth "bag" and allow the whey (WATER RESIDUE) to drain away. Salt to taste.

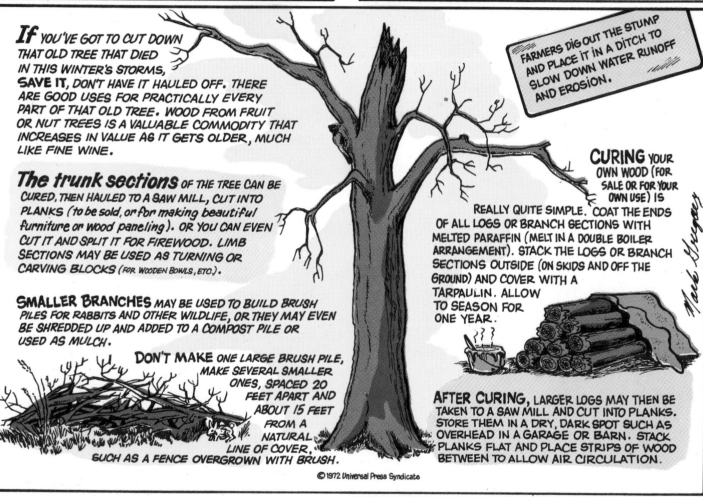

If YOU'VE GOT TO CUT DOWN THAT OLD TREE THAT DIED IN THIS WINTER'S STORMS, **SAVE IT,** DON'T HAVE IT HAULED OFF. THERE ARE GOOD USES FOR PRACTICALLY EVERY PART OF THAT OLD TREE. WOOD FROM FRUIT OR NUT TREES IS A VALUABLE COMMODITY THAT INCREASES IN VALUE AS IT GETS OLDER, MUCH LIKE FINE WINE.

The trunk sections OF THE TREE CAN BE CURED, THEN HAULED TO A SAW MILL, CUT INTO PLANKS (to be sold, or for making beautiful furniture or wood paneling). OR YOU CAN EVEN CUT IT AND SPLIT IT FOR FIREWOOD. LIMB SECTIONS MAY BE USED AS TURNING OR CARVING BLOCKS (FOR WOODEN BOWLS, ETC.).

SMALLER BRANCHES MAY BE USED TO BUILD BRUSH PILES FOR RABBITS AND OTHER WILDLIFE, OR THEY MAY EVEN BE SHREDDED UP AND ADDED TO A COMPOST PILE OR USED AS MULCH.

DON'T MAKE ONE LARGE BRUSH PILE, MAKE SEVERAL SMALLER ONES, SPACED 20 FEET APART AND ABOUT 15 FEET FROM A NATURAL LINE OF COVER, SUCH AS A FENCE OVERGROWN WITH BRUSH.

FARMERS DIG OUT THE STUMP AND PLACE IT IN A DITCH TO SLOW DOWN WATER RUNOFF AND EROSION.

CURING YOUR OWN WOOD (FOR SALE OR FOR YOUR OWN USE) IS REALLY QUITE SIMPLE. COAT THE ENDS OF ALL LOGS OR BRANCH SECTIONS WITH MELTED PARAFFIN (MELT IN A DOUBLE BOILER ARRANGEMENT). STACK THE LOGS OR BRANCH SECTIONS OUTSIDE (ON SKIDS AND OFF THE GROUND) AND COVER WITH A TARPAULIN. ALLOW TO SEASON FOR ONE YEAR.

AFTER CURING, LARGER LOGS MAY THEN BE TAKEN TO A SAW MILL AND CUT INTO PLANKS. STORE THEM IN A DRY, DARK SPOT SUCH AS OVERHEAD IN A GARAGE OR BARN. STACK PLANKS FLAT AND PLACE STRIPS OF WOOD BETWEEN TO ALLOW AIR CIRCULATION.

© 1972 Universal Press Syndicate

Natural Crafts

A FAVORITE DRINKING CUP OF INDIANS and FRONTIERSMAN ALIKE WAS THE "NOGGIN" MUG. IT WAS MADE FROM A BURL or "KNOT" CUT FROM A DEAD TREE.

STEP 1. SAW OFF THE LUMP, LEAVING A HANDLE PORTION AS SHOWN.

SAW ON THIS LINE

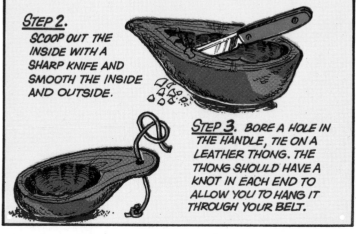

STEP 2. SCOOP OUT THE INSIDE WITH A SHARP KNIFE AND SMOOTH THE INSIDE AND OUTSIDE.

STEP 3. BORE A HOLE IN THE HANDLE, TIE ON A LEATHER THONG. THE THONG SHOULD HAVE A KNOT IN EACH END TO ALLOW YOU TO HANG IT THROUGH YOUR BELT.

FOREST EDGE and FOREST CLEARINGS, WITH A VARIETY OF PLANTS, ARE USUALLY IDEAL ANIMAL HABITAT.

WILDLIFE CANNOT BE STOCKPILED. THE NUMBERS OF ANIMALS OR BIRDS ON A GIVEN AREA CAN BE INCREASED ONLY UP TO WHAT THE LAND WILL SUPPORT, THEN OVERPOPULATION RESULTS --WITH ALL ITS PROBLEMS.

"ACRES FOR WILDLIFE" IS A NEW CONSERVATION PROGRAM THAT EVERYONE CAN HELP. THE PROGRAM IS AN ANSWER TO THE DILEMMA WILDLIFE FACES DUE TO SHRINKING HABITAT AS MORE AND MORE LAND IS GOBBLED UP FOR SUBURBAN HOUSING TRACTS, SHOPPING CENTERS and HIGHWAYS, AND AS MORE AND MORE FARMERS PRACTICE "CLEAN FARMING" OR THE BULL-DOZING OFF OF ALL BRUSH AND TREES TO PLACE MORE OF THEIR VALUABLE ACRES IN CROPLAND PRODUCTION.

THE "ACRES FOR WILDLIFE" PLAN IS SIMPLE. FARMERS AND OTHER LANDOWNERS ARE ASKED TO ENROLL TRACTS OF THEIR PROPERTY, ONE ACRE OR LARGER IN SIZE, AND TO PRESERVE THESE TRACTS FROM GRAZING, BURNING, MOWING and SPRAYING FOR AT LEAST A YEAR.

ALMOST EVERY FARM OR RANCH HAS AREAS THAT ARE NOT SUITED FOR AGRICULTURE WITH POTENTIAL FOR THIS PURPOSE. THESE INCLUDE SMALL WOODLOTS, HARD-TO-CULTIVATE SECTIONS, DITCHES AND FENCE LINES, OR SWAMPS AND MARSHES. THE DEDICATION OF SUCH LAND TO THE "ACRES FOR WILDLIFE" PROGRAM DOES NOT INVOLVE ANY ECONOMIC LOSS TO THE LANDOWNERS.

THE PARTICIPATING LANDOWNERS RECEIVE A SPECIAL CERTIFICATE AS WELL AS LARGE SIGNS FOR POSTING ON LAND ENROLLED IN THE PROGRAM.

EVEN IF YOU AREN'T A LANDOWNER, HERE IS A WAY YOU CAN HELP: GET OUT AND SCOUT SUCH LAND. ASK FARMERS AND LANDOWNERS TO ENROLL SOME OF THEIR UNUSED ACRES. INDIVIDUALS WHO HAVE HELPED ENROLL LAND PLOTS RECEIVE A "WILDLIFE AIDE" CERTIFICATE. ORGANIZATIONS WHO SIGN UP A SIGNIFICANT NUMBER OF ACRES ARE GIVEN A "FRIENDS OF WILDLIFE" CITATION.

FOR MORE INFORMATION ON "ACRES FOR WILDLIFE" CONTACT YOUR LOCAL GAME AND FISH DEPARTMENT, LOCAL COUNTY AGENT, EXTENSION OFFICE, OR SOIL CONSERVATION SERVICE.

Mort Gregory

Natural Crafts

GOOD WILDLIFE HABITAT CONSISTS OF THREE ELEMENTS:

- FOOD
- WATER
- COVER or SHELTER

JANUARY

January is the month of planning, a time to spend poring over seed catalogs and dreaming of that first taste of crispy lettuce, or sugar-sweet peas simmered with fresh new little potatoes scrubbed clean and dropped whole in the pot.

January is not a time of laziness, however — there's lots to be done. The garden rakes, hoes, shovels have to be gathered and cleaned and fixed up. All garden utensils should be scraped clean of mud and given a light coating of rust-protecting oil. January is a cruel month on wildlife, and a time when you can help.

Bird feeders placed strategically will help many small birds make it through the winter. But remember—you must attend to them every day and keep food in them; the birds will begin to depend on you to provide food for them.

FEBRUARY

Take your seed packets in hand, for February is the month to start such plants as tomatoes and peppers indoors in seed flats; later you'll transplant them into cold frames or the garden.

February is also the month to clean and fix up your fishing tackle. Now's the time to tie new flies, repaint plugs, oil reels and repair rods. In some parts of the country you can start cleaning up last year's garden and start getting ready for this year's planting.

February is also a good time to locate a good supply of dried cow manure to be used as fertilizer for the year's garden.

February is also a time for short walks in the woods. The landscape seems desolate and dead, yet you know that within a matter of weeks it will all change completely with a new life.

MARCH

March is a favorite month with many country people because it brings out the first of the greens, those wild plants that are so delicious cooked or even raw in salads. The countryside is literally covered with the fresh young shoots and leaves of such plants as curley and slick dock, pokeweed, lambs quarter and shepherds purse. Get to know these plants well and you'll have a delicious and healthful spring.

You can start putting out such plants as cabbage, onions, potatoes, beets, carrots, cauliflower in the garden, and begin to transplant some other plants from the cold frame into the garden.

APRIL

By April almost any plant, whether tender or hardy, can be planted or transplanted into the garden. April is also a good time to tend to your fruit orchards, removing any animal-protection bands from trees, and adding much mulch around the root system if needed. April is a month for long walks in the woods, as all the wildflowers are beginning to show their colors to welcome the spring in full swing.

Some of the later wild greens are just starting to come up in quantities, and it's a good time for gathering a big mess of greens to freeze for the following winter.

MAY

The month of May produces one of the best excuses for tramping the woods. Now is the time to search for one of nature's most delicious plants—mushrooms. From about the last week in April through most of May, these mysterious plants start popping up. A warm sunny afternoon following a spring shower, a favorite hunting time for knowledgeable mushroomers, can seem to make these plants appear almost like magic.

May is also the time to watch the garden closely, making sure all the young plants get started properly; and it's a time for some good old honest hoeing.

JUNE

Almost any month is a great time to go fishing,
but June is the most pleasant. A warm June night
spent slumbering by your favorite stream or
fishing hole after a meal of fresh-fried fish is
something dreams are made of. Of course, to be
able to spend more time fishing, you'll have
to give the garden a little something special.
A good layer of hay or leaf mulch applied between
rows will help hold in moisture and prevent
weeds, giving you more time for fishing and
a lot less hoeing.

JULY

July is the month of hot summer days and mouth-watering blackberry cobblers. Watch your favorite berry patch, whether it's blackberries, raspberries or the huge delicious dew berries. These berries can ripen almost overnight in the long sunny days, and if you don't hurry the birds will beat you to all of them.

But if you do beat the birds to the patch, be generous, and leave some for them too. There will be plenty until someone decides to bulldoze off the brush, and make way for more housing or for more cattle-grazing.

AUGUST

August is a month of work, as the fruits of your earlier labors become ready for picking, preparing and storing for the next winter. You'll spend lots of time canning and freezing. August is a good month to start planting some late plants for winter use — turnips, parsnips and carrots.

Remember to start saving seeds from this year's vegetables and flowers for use in next year's garden.

SEPTEMBER

There's still plenty of work to do in the garden, what with gathering and storing lots of goodies. September is also a good time to start compost heaps. Start gathering leaves as soon as they fall and place them in piles covered with old tarpaulins near the garden. Areas of the garden that are idle should be covered with sheet compost consisting of well-dried cow manure and old straw or leaves.

September is also a good time to tend to the orchard, wrapping the young trees with paper to keep rabbits from chewing off the bark. Add more old hay as a mulch around the base of the young trees, but pull it back a few inches away from the trunk to avoid providing a runway for mice.

OCTOBER

The nights are beginning to get nippy and it's time to collect the firewood. You'll need to gather a lot of wood if you have a fireplace and a cook-stove too, but this is one of the most rewarding of jobs. As the old timers say, "Gathering firewood gives two heats, one when you cut it and carry it in and one when you burn it."

Keep your eyes on the hickory nuts, because they'll be ready to pick off the ground almost overnight, and when they're ready almost every squirrel in the country will be there waiting for them. But if you're observant you may steal enough for a hickory-nut pie or for some Christmas candy.

NOVEMBER

All the nut trees are dropping nuts by now, and you can easily gather baskets of pecans, walnuts and hickories. Pour them all out in the backyard and let the weather help you remove the husks. With a big pile of husked and cleaned nuts, you've got a welcome task ahead when the winter wind starts to whistle. A cozy fireplace and the quietness brought on by the concentration needed to pick out nutmeats make a welcome respite from the hurried work of fall.

DECEMBER

Winter is in full swing, and before the hard freeze sets in, turnips and other root crops should be gathered and stored in the root cellar or in sawdust or straw in boxes in the basement.

When white fluffy snow covers the ground, take long walks and observe the daily life of the animals and birds around you. You'll see the random wandering tracks of a rabbit as he wanders looking for a blade of grass or some tender-barked tree, or perhaps the spot where tiny birds have scratched in the snow to reveal some frozen grasses. You might even spot a set of whitetail deer tracks leading off to some mysterious rendezvous.

INDEX